THE SOCCER DIET

PEAK PERFORMANCE FOR ATHLETES
INCLUDES 80 COMPLETE RECIPES

BY:
KEVIN KULLMAN

Copyright

The Soccer Diet

Peak Performance for Athletes

Includes 80 Complete Recipes

Text by Kevin Kullman

All rights reserved. No part of this publication may be reproduced, distributed, or transmitted in any form or by any means, or stored in a database or retrieval system, without the prior permission of the publisher.

First e-book edition 2023

Table of Contents

ABOUT THE AUTHOR 1

CHAPTER 1: Why is a Healthy Diet so Important 3

CHAPTER 2: Best Foods the Day Before a Game 7

    Recipe: Grilled Chicken Breast with Brown Rice and Steamed Vegetables: 9

    Recipe: Quinoa Salad with Grilled Shrimp, Mixed Vegetables, and a Citrus Vinaigrette Dressing: 10

    Recipe: Whole Wheat Pasta with Tomato Sauce, Grilled Chicken, and Spinach: 12

    Recipe: Grilled Salmon with Sweet Potato Mash and Green Beans: 13

    Recipe: Turkey and Vegetable Stir-Fry with Brown Rice: 15

    Recipe: Baked Sweet Potato with Black Beans, Avocado, and Salsa: 17

    Recipe: Grilled Flank Steak with Roasted Sweet Potato Wedges and Sautéed Kale: 18

    Recipe: Lentil Soup with Mixed Vegetables and Whole Wheat Bread: 19

    Recipe: Grilled Tofu with Mixed Vegetables and Brown Rice: 21

    Recipe: Broiled White Fish with Mixed Vegetables and Roasted Red Potatoes: 22

CHAPTER 3: Best Foods Right Before a Game 24

    Recipe: Banana and Peanut Butter Toast 27

    Recipe: Greek Yogurt with Fruits and Nuts 27

    Recipe: Oatmeal with Fruit and Almonds 28

 Recipe: Whole Wheat Turkey Sandwich 29

 Recipe: Whole Wheat Bagel with Cream Cheese and Smoked Salmon 30

 Recipe: Turkey and Cheese Wrap...31

 Recipe: Grilled Chicken and Vegetable Skewers 32

 Recipe: Brown Rice and Grilled Shrimp Bowl........................33

 Recipe: Grilled Shrimp Tacos..35

 Recipe: Hard Boiled Eggs and Fruit 36

CHAPTER 4: Best Foods During a Game................................38

 Sports Drinks..39

 Energy Gels...40

 Bananas 41

 Energy Bars...42

 Sandwiches...43

CHAPTER 5: Best Foods After a Game.....................................45

 Recipe: Grilled Turkey Burger, Roasted Sweet Potato Wedges and a Side Salad with Mixed Greens 47

 Recipe: Quinoa and Black Bean Salad with Roasted Vegetables and a Lemon Vinaigrette...49

 Recipe: Grilled Salmon with Roasted Sweet Potatoes and Steamed Asparagus 51

 Recipe: Whole Wheat Pita with Hummus, Grilled Chicken, and Mixed Vegetables 52

 Recipe: Grilled Flank Steak with Roasted Root Vegetables and Sautéed Spinach: 53

 Recipe: Tuna and Mixed Vegetable Salad with a Citrus Vinaigrette Dressing 54

 Recipe: Brown Rice Bowl with Grilled Tofu, Mixed Vegetables, and a Peanut Sauce..55

 Recipe: Baked Sweet Potato with Black Beans, Salsa, and Greek Yogurt 56

 Recipe: Turkey and Vegetable Stir-Fry with Brown Rice.........57

Recipe: Grilled Shrimp Skewers with Quinoa Salad 58
CHAPTER 6: Snacks 61
   Recipe: Fruit and Nut Butter 62
   Recipe: Greek Yogurt and Berries 63
   Recipe: Hard-Boiled Eggs 64
   Recipe: Trail Mix 65
   Recipe: Hummus and Vegetables 66
   Recipe: Rice Cakes with Avocado and Turkey 67
   Recipe: Smoothie 67
   Recipe: Cottage Cheese and Fruit 68
   Recipe: Energy Balls 69
   Recipe: Roasted Chickpeas 70
CHAPTER 7: Breakfast 72
   Recipe: Protein Pancakes 74
   Recipe: Greek Yogurt Parfait 75
   Recipe: Egg and Veggie Scramble 76
   Recipe: Avocado Toast 77
   Recipe: Overnight Oats 78
   Recipe: Breakfast Burrito 79
   Recipe: Smoothie Bowl 80
   Recipe: Veggie Omelet 81
   Recipe: Protein Waffles 82
   Recipe: Cottage Cheese and Fruit 83
CHAPTER 8: Lunch 85
   Recipe: Grilled Chicken Sandwich 87
   Recipe: Grilled Chicken Caesar Salad 88
   Recipe: Tuna Salad Wrap 90
   Recipe: Avocado and Egg Salad 91
   Recipe: Chicken Burrito Bowl 92
   Recipe: Veggie Burger 93

Recipe: Turkey Chili 95

Recipe: Salmon Caesar Salad 97

Recipe: Grilled Vegetable Panini 98

Recipe: Baked Sweet Potato 99

CHAPTER 9: Dinner 101

Recipe: Grilled Chicken Breast with Roasted Brussels Sprouts and Brown Rice 104

Recipe: Spaghetti Squash with Turkey Meatballs and Marinara Sauce 105

Recipe: Turkey and Vegetable Chili with Brown Rice 106

Recipe: Baked Cod with Steamed Vegetables 107

Recipe: Egg and Vegetable Scramble 109

Recipe: Grilled Chicken and Pineapple Skewers 110

Recipe: Grilled Steak with Baked Potatoes and Green Beans . 111

Recipe: Greek-Style Chicken Salad with Whole Wheat Pita .. 113

Recipe: Shrimp and Broccoli Stir-Fry 114

Recipe: Shrimp and Avocado Salad 115

CHAPTER 10: Desserts 117

Recipe: Fruit Salad with a Drizzle of Honey or a Dollop of Greek Yogurt 118

Recipe: Frozen Banana Bites Dipped in Dark Chocolate and Sprinkled with Nuts or Coconut 119

Recipe: Baked Apples Topped with Cinnamon and a Sprinkle of Granola 120

Recipe: Chia Seed Pudding Made with Almond Milk and Topped with Fresh Berries 121

Recipe: Berry Sorbet Made with Frozen Berries and a Splash of Coconut Water 121

Recipe: Avocado Chocolate Mousse Made with Ripe Avocado, Cocoa Powder, and Honey 122

Recipe: Greek Yogurt Parfait with Layers of Fruit and Granola 123

Recipe: Homemade Fruit Popsicles Made with Pureed Fruit and Coconut Water 124

Recipe: Baked Pears with a Drizzle of Maple Syrup and a Sprinkle of Cinnamon 124

Recipe: A Small Serving of Dark Chocolate with a Handful of Almonds or Walnuts 125

CONCLUSION: 127

ABOUT THE AUTHOR

Kevin Kullman is a life-long soccer player, coach, fan and parent with a desire to share his passion and knowledge of this game with others.

He grew up in the small town of Mount Pleasant, Michigan. Kevin's unique perspective as someone who grew up in a town dominated by other sports gives him a valuable insight into the challenges faced by those who love soccer but may not have the resources or support to pursue it. Through his writing, he seeks to provide encouragement and guidance to those who share his passion for the beautiful game.

As a child he excelled in multiple sports including soccer, football, basketball and tennis. However the small town lacked the necessary coaches, training facilities or passion for specializing in the sport of soccer. During his adolescent years the true love of the game was brought out by his High School soccer coach.

Kevin began his soccer coaching career at age 18 and continued to play club soccer throughout his college years. After college he moved to South Florida and continued his coaching career as a high-school teacher and Varsity soccer coach. He led his team to numerous winning seasons and the Florida High School State Championships as well as developing multiple college athletes.

Kevin left teaching to pursue other opportunities but has continued to coach and train youth players in the South Florida area. He focuses heavily on training his two children Erika and Jordan who both play competitive youth soccer. He believes strongly that peak performance must include a focus on diet. This book provides parents, players and coaches an easy to follow diet plan for soccer athletes.

CHAPTER 1:
WHY IS A HEALTHY DIET SO IMPORTANT

The physical demands of soccer require players to engage in both aerobic and anaerobic activities throughout the game, such as running, sprinting, jumping, tackling, and changing direction. These activities require a lot of energy, which is primarily provided by carbohydrates stored in the body as glycogen. As glycogen levels decrease, the body starts to burn stored fat as an energy source, leading to an increase in calorie expenditure. Studies suggest that the average soccer player can burn between 500 to 1000 calories during a 90-minute match.

It is important to note that the number of calories burned during a soccer match is just an estimate and can vary from player to player. It is also essential to replenish the lost calories by consuming a balanced diet that includes carbohydrates, protein, and healthy fats, along with adequate hydration before, during, and after the game.

Soccer players burn a significant number of calories during a match due to the high-intensity physical demands of the sport. The number of calories burned can vary depending on several factors such as age, weight, height, fitness level, and intensity of the game. It is crucial for soccer players to consume a balanced diet and hydrate properly to replenish lost calories and maintain optimal performance during training and matches.

Competitive soccer players require a combination of physical and nutritional needs to maintain optimal performance during training and games. The physical demands of soccer are intense, requiring players to have a high level of aerobic and anaerobic fitness, strength, power, and agility. Here are some of the essential physical and nutritional needs for professional soccer players:

Aerobic Fitness: Professional soccer players need excellent aerobic fitness to run for long distances throughout the match. Aerobic fitness can be developed through endurance training such as long-distance running, cycling, and swimming.

Anaerobic Fitness: In soccer, players often need to make short sprints, changes in direction, and sudden stops. This requires good anaerobic fitness. High-intensity interval training (HIIT) is an effective way to improve anaerobic fitness.

Strength and Power: Soccer players need strength and power to perform various actions such as kicking, jumping, and tackling. Strength training exercises such as squats, deadlifts, and lunges can help improve leg strength, while upper body strength can be improved through exercises such as bench press and pull-ups.

Agility: Soccer players need to be agile and able to change direction quickly. Agility drills such as shuttle runs, cone drills, and ladder drills can help improve agility.

Hydration: Professional soccer players need to stay hydrated before, during, and after matches. They should drink plenty of water and electrolyte-rich sports drinks to replace fluids lost through sweat.

Balanced Nutrition: A balanced diet that includes carbohydrates, protein, and healthy fats is essential for professional soccer players. Carbohydrates are the primary energy source for high-intensity exercise, while protein helps repair and rebuild muscles. Healthy fats are also essential for energy and overall health.

Timing of Meals: Soccer players should time their meals and snacks appropriately to ensure that they have enough energy to perform at their best during training and games. Pre-match meals should be consumed three to four hours before the game, while snacks should be eaten 30 minutes to an hour before the game.

Soccer is a physically demanding sport that requires a lot of energy and endurance. To perform at their best on the field, soccer players need to fuel their bodies with nutritious food that provides them with the necessary nutrients and energy to sustain high-intensity activity for extended periods. Eating a healthy diet is crucial for soccer players for several reasons, including:

Improved Performance: Eating a healthy diet can help soccer players improve their performance on the field. Nutritious foods provide the body with the energy, vitamins, minerals, and other essential nutrients it needs to perform at its best. By eating a balanced diet, soccer players can improve their strength, speed, and endurance, allowing them to perform at peak levels for longer periods.

Faster Recovery: Soccer players need to be able to recover quickly after games and training sessions. A healthy diet that includes foods high in protein and other nutrients can help speed up the recovery process, reducing the risk of injury and allowing players to get back on the field sooner.

Reduced Risk of Injury: Eating a healthy diet can also reduce the risk of injury in soccer players. Nutritious foods provide the body with the nutrients it needs to repair and maintain muscle and bone tissue, making it less susceptible to injuries. Additionally, a healthy diet can help maintain a healthy weight, reducing the risk of strain and injury to joints and muscles.

Increased Mental Focus: Eating a healthy diet can also improve mental focus and clarity, which is crucial for soccer players. Nutritious foods provide the brain with the energy and nutrients it needs to function at its best, allowing players to stay focused and alert during games and training sessions.

Improved Overall Health: Finally, eating a healthy diet can improve overall health and wellbeing, reducing the risk of chronic illnesses such as heart disease, diabetes, and obesity. Soccer players who prioritize their health and wellbeing by eating a balanced diet can enjoy a longer, healthier, and more fulfilling life both on and off the field.

In conclusion, eating a healthy diet is crucial for soccer players looking to perform at their best on the field. A balanced diet provides the body with the energy and nutrients it needs to improve performance, speed up recovery, reduce the risk of injury, improve mental focus, and enhance overall health and wellbeing. By making healthy food choices, soccer players can take their game to the next level and enjoy a long, successful career in the sport.

CHAPTER 2:
BEST FOODS THE DAY BEFORE A GAME

What you eat the day before a soccer game can have a significant impact on your performance. Here are some of the best foods to eat the day before a soccer game:

Whole grain pasta: Whole grain pasta is a great source of complex carbohydrates, which can help to provide a sustained source of energy during the game. It's also easy to digest, making it a good choice for the day before the game.

Brown rice: Brown rice is another great source of complex carbohydrates. It's also high in fiber and nutrients, which can help to support overall health and well-being.

Lean protein: Eating lean protein, such as grilled chicken or fish, can help to support muscle growth and repair. It's important to choose lean sources of protein to avoid consuming too much saturated fat.

Vegetables: Vegetables are an important source of nutrients, such as vitamins, minerals, and fiber. Eating a variety of colorful vegetables can help to support overall health and well-being, which can in turn support performance during the game.

Fruit: Fruit is a great source of carbohydrates and can help to provide a quick source of energy. It's also high in vitamins and minerals, which can help to support overall health and well-being.

Nuts and seeds: Nuts and seeds are a good source of healthy fats, which can help to support brain function and overall health. They can also provide a quick source of energy and help to keep you feeling full and satisfied.

It's important to avoid consuming too much saturated fat, sugar, or alcohol in the day before the game, as these can have a negative impact on performance. Additionally, it's important to stay hydrated by drinking plenty of water throughout the day.

10 Recipes for Soccer Players to Eat the Day Before a Game:

1. Grilled chicken breast with brown rice and steamed vegetables
2. Quinoa salad with grilled shrimp, mixed vegetables, and a citrus vinaigrette dressing
3. Whole wheat pasta with tomato sauce, grilled chicken, and spinach
4. Grilled salmon with sweet potato mash and green beans
5. Turkey and vegetable stir-fry with brown rice
6. Baked sweet potato with black beans, avocado, and salsa
7. Grilled flank steak with roasted sweet potato wedges and sautéed kale
8. Lentil soup with mixed vegetables and whole wheat bread
9. Grilled tofu with mixed vegetables and brown rice

10. Broiled white fish with mixed vegetables and roasted red potatoes

These recipes include a variety of nutrient-dense ingredients, such as lean protein, complex carbohydrates, and vegetables. They also provide a good balance of macronutrients and fiber to support energy levels and digestion. Remember to also drink plenty of water and avoid foods that may upset your stomach or cause discomfort.

Recipe: Grilled Chicken Breast with Brown Rice and Steamed Vegetables:

Ingredients:

- 4 boneless, skinless chicken breasts
- 1 cup brown rice
- 2 cups water
- 2 tablespoons olive oil
- 2 cloves garlic, minced
- Salt and pepper, to taste
- 2 cups mixed vegetables (such as broccoli, carrots, and bell peppers)
- Lemon wedges, for serving

Instructions:

1. Preheat grill to medium-high heat.
2. In a medium saucepan, combine the brown rice, water, and a pinch of salt. Bring to a boil, then reduce the heat to low and simmer, covered, until the rice is tender and the water is absorbed, about 40-45 minutes.

3. While the rice is cooking, prepare the chicken. Brush the chicken breasts with olive oil, then season with minced garlic, salt, and pepper.

4. Place the chicken on the grill and cook for 6-8 minutes per side, or until cooked through and no longer pink in the middle.

5. While the chicken is cooking, steam the mixed vegetables in a separate pot or steamer basket for 4-5 minutes, or until tender but still slightly crisp.

6. To serve, divide the brown rice among four plates. Add a portion of steamed vegetables on top of the rice, and place a grilled chicken breast on top of the vegetables. Garnish with lemon wedges and enjoy!

This recipe provides a balance of lean protein, complex carbohydrates, and fiber from the brown rice and mixed vegetables. It is also easy to customize by swapping out the vegetables or seasoning the chicken with your favorite herbs and spices.

Recipe: Quinoa Salad with Grilled Shrimp, Mixed Vegetables, and a Citrus Vinaigrette Dressing:

Ingredients:

- 1 cup quinoa, rinsed
- 2 cups water
- 1 pound large shrimp, peeled and deveined
- 2 tablespoons olive oil
- 1 teaspoon paprika
- 1/2 teaspoon garlic powder

- Salt and pepper, to taste
- 2 cups mixed vegetables (such as bell peppers, cucumber, and cherry tomatoes)
- 1/4 cup chopped fresh parsley
- 1/4 cup chopped fresh mint
- 1/4 cup chopped fresh cilantro
- For the dressing:
- 1/4 cup olive oil
- 2 tablespoons fresh lemon juice
- 1 tablespoon fresh orange juice
- 1 tablespoon honey
- 1 teaspoon Dijon mustard
- Salt and pepper, to taste

Instructions:

1. In a medium saucepan, combine the quinoa and water. Bring to a boil, then reduce the heat to low and simmer, covered, until the quinoa is tender and the water is absorbed, about 15-20 minutes. Set aside to cool.
2. Preheat grill to medium-high heat.
3. In a small bowl, whisk together the olive oil, paprika, garlic powder, salt, and pepper. Toss the shrimp in the mixture to coat.
4. Place the shrimp on the grill and cook for 2-3 minutes per side, or until pink and cooked through.

5. While the shrimp is cooking, prepare the mixed vegetables by chopping them into bite-sized pieces.

6. In a large bowl, combine the cooked quinoa, mixed vegetables, chopped herbs, and grilled shrimp.

7. To make the dressing, whisk together the olive oil, lemon juice, orange juice, honey, Dijon mustard, salt, and pepper in a small bowl.

8. Drizzle the dressing over the quinoa salad and toss to coat evenly.

9. Serve the salad immediately or refrigerate until ready to eat.

This recipe is packed with protein from the shrimp and quinoa, as well as vitamins and minerals from the mixed vegetables and fresh herbs. The citrus vinaigrette dressing adds a tangy and sweet flavor that complements the other ingredients perfectly.

Recipe: Whole Wheat Pasta with Tomato Sauce, Grilled Chicken, and Spinach:

Ingredients:

- 8 ounces whole wheat pasta
- 2 boneless, skinless chicken breasts
- 1 tablespoon olive oil
- Salt and pepper, to taste
- 2 cups tomato sauce (homemade or store-bought)
- 2 cups baby spinach leaves
- 1/4 cup grated Parmesan cheese

Instructions:

1. Cook the pasta according to package instructions in a large pot of salted boiling water until al dente. Drain and set aside.
2. Preheat grill to medium-high heat.
3. Brush the chicken breasts with olive oil and season with salt and pepper.
4. Grill the chicken for 6-8 minutes per side, or until cooked through and no longer pink in the middle. Let the chicken rest for a few minutes before slicing into thin strips.
5. In a large saucepan, heat the tomato sauce over medium heat until warmed through.
6. Add the cooked pasta, sliced chicken, and baby spinach to the saucepan. Toss everything together until the pasta is coated in the tomato sauce and the spinach is wilted.
7. Divide the pasta and chicken mixture among four plates. Sprinkle with grated Parmesan cheese and serve immediately.

This recipe is a great source of complex carbohydrates, lean protein, and fiber from the whole wheat pasta, grilled chicken, and spinach. The tomato sauce adds antioxidants and vitamins, while the Parmesan cheese provides a source of calcium. You can also customize this recipe by adding other vegetables or herbs to the tomato sauce, such as bell peppers or basil.

Recipe: Grilled Salmon with Sweet Potato Mash and Green Beans:

Ingredients:

- 4 salmon fillets
- 1 tablespoon olive oil
- Salt and pepper, to taste
- 4 medium sweet potatoes, peeled and cubed
- 2 tablespoons butter
- 1/4 cup milk
- 1/4 teaspoon cinnamon
- 1/4 teaspoon nutmeg
- 1 pound green beans, trimmed
- 1 tablespoon balsamic vinegar

Instructions:

1. Preheat grill to medium-high heat.
2. Brush the salmon fillets with olive oil and season with salt and pepper.
3. Grill the salmon for 3-4 minutes per side, or until cooked through and flaky.
4. While the salmon is cooking, prepare the sweet potato mash by boiling the sweet potato cubes in a large pot of salted water until tender, about 15-20 minutes. Drain the sweet potatoes and return them to the pot.
5. Add the butter, milk, cinnamon, and nutmeg to the pot. Mash the sweet potatoes with a potato masher or fork until smooth and creamy.
6. In a separate pot, blanch the green beans in boiling salted water for 3-4 minutes, or until bright green and

tender-crisp. Drain and toss with balsamic vinegar.

7. Divide the sweet potato mash and green beans among four plates. Top each plate with a grilled salmon fillet.

This recipe is a great source of heart-healthy omega-3 fatty acids from the salmon, as well as complex carbohydrates, fiber, and beta-carotene from the sweet potatoes. The green beans provide a source of vitamins and minerals, and the balsamic vinegar adds a tangy and sweet flavor to the dish. You can also substitute other types of fish or vegetables depending on your preferences.

Recipe: Turkey and Vegetable Stir-Fry with Brown Rice:

Ingredients:

- 1 pound ground turkey
- 1 tablespoon vegetable oil
- 2 cloves garlic, minced
- 1 tablespoon grated ginger
- 1 red bell pepper, sliced
- 1 green bell pepper, sliced
- 1 small onion, sliced
- 2 cups broccoli florets
- 1 cup sliced mushrooms
- 2 tablespoons soy sauce
- 1 tablespoon rice vinegar

- 1 teaspoon honey
- Salt and pepper, to taste
- 4 cups cooked brown rice

Instructions:

1. Heat the vegetable oil in a large skillet over medium-high heat.
2. Add the ground turkey to the skillet and cook for 5-6 minutes, breaking up the meat with a wooden spoon, until no longer pink.
3. Add the garlic and ginger to the skillet and cook for 1-2 minutes, until fragrant.
4. Add the sliced bell peppers, onion, broccoli, and mushrooms to the skillet. Cook for 5-6 minutes, stirring occasionally, until the vegetables are tender.
5. In a small bowl, whisk together the soy sauce, rice vinegar, honey, salt, and pepper.
6. Pour the soy sauce mixture over the turkey and vegetables in the skillet. Toss everything together until the sauce is evenly distributed.
7. Serve the stir-fry over brown rice.

This recipe is a great source of lean protein from the turkey, as well as a variety of vitamins and minerals from the vegetables. The brown rice provides complex carbohydrates and fiber, while the soy sauce adds a savory and umami flavor to the dish. You can also customize this recipe by using different types of vegetables or adding in other ingredients like cashews or water chestnuts for added texture.

Recipe: Baked Sweet Potato with Black Beans, Avocado, and Salsa:

Ingredients:

- 4 medium sweet potatoes
- 1 can black beans, drained and rinsed
- 1 avocado, diced
- 1/2 cup salsa
- 1/4 cup chopped fresh cilantro
- Salt and pepper, to taste

Instructions:

1. Preheat the oven to 400°F (200°C).
2. Wash and scrub the sweet potatoes. Pierce each potato with a fork a few times.
3. Place the sweet potatoes on a baking sheet and bake for 45-60 minutes, or until tender when pierced with a fork.
4. In a small saucepan, heat the black beans over medium heat until warmed through.
5. When the sweet potatoes are done, remove them from the oven and let them cool for a few minutes.
6. Slice each sweet potato lengthwise and use a fork to fluff the flesh inside.
7. Divide the black beans among the sweet potatoes. Top each sweet potato with diced avocado, salsa, and chopped cilantro.
8. Season with salt and pepper to taste.

This recipe is a great source of complex carbohydrates and fiber from the sweet potatoes and black beans, as well as heart-healthy fats from the avocado. The salsa adds a fresh and tangy flavor to the dish, while the cilantro adds a burst of herbaceousness. You can also add other toppings like shredded cheese or sour cream, depending on your preferences.

Recipe: Grilled Flank Steak with Roasted Sweet Potato Wedges and Sautéed Kale:

Ingredients:

- 1 lb flank steak
- 2 large sweet potatoes, cut into wedges
- 1 bunch kale, stems removed and chopped
- 2 tablespoons olive oil
- 1 tablespoon balsamic vinegar
- 2 cloves garlic, minced
- Salt and pepper, to taste

Instructions:

1. Preheat the grill to high heat.
2. Season the flank steak with salt and pepper on both sides.
3. Place the steak on the grill and cook for 4-5 minutes per side, or until desired doneness is reached.
4. While the steak is cooking, preheat the oven to 400°F (200°C). Place the sweet potato wedges on a baking sheet and drizzle with 1 tablespoon of olive oil. Season with salt and pepper, and roast in the oven for 20-25 minutes, or

until tender and crispy.

5. In a large skillet, heat the remaining tablespoon of olive oil over medium heat. Add the garlic and cook for 1-2 minutes, until fragrant.
6. Add the chopped kale to the skillet and toss to coat with the oil and garlic. Cook for 5-7 minutes, stirring occasionally, until the kale is wilted and tender.
7. Drizzle the sautéed kale with balsamic vinegar and season with salt and pepper to taste.
8. Let the steak rest for a few minutes before slicing it against the grain.
9. Serve the grilled flank steak with roasted sweet potato wedges and sautéed kale on the side.

This recipe is a great source of lean protein from the flank steak, as well as complex carbohydrates and fiber from the sweet potatoes and kale. The balsamic vinegar adds a tangy and slightly sweet flavor to the kale, while the garlic adds a savory depth of flavor. You can also add other seasonings to the sweet potato wedges, such as paprika or cinnamon, for added flavor.

Recipe: Lentil Soup with Mixed Vegetables and Whole Wheat Bread:

Ingredients:

- 1 cup dried lentils, rinsed and drained
- 1 onion, chopped
- 3 cloves garlic, minced
- 2 stalks celery, chopped

- 2 carrots, chopped
- 1 zucchini, chopped
- 4 cups vegetable broth
- 1 tablespoon olive oil
- 1 teaspoon dried thyme
- Salt and pepper, to taste
- Whole wheat bread, for serving

Instructions:

1. In a large pot, heat the olive oil over medium heat. Add the onion, garlic, celery, and carrots, and sauté for 5-7 minutes, or until the vegetables are tender.
2. Add the zucchini to the pot and sauté for another 2-3 minutes.
3. Add the lentils, vegetable broth, dried thyme, salt, and pepper to the pot. Bring to a boil, then reduce the heat and let simmer for 30-35 minutes, or until the lentils are tender.
4. Use an immersion blender or transfer the soup to a blender and blend until smooth.
5. Serve the soup hot with a slice of whole wheat bread on the side.

This recipe is a great source of plant-based protein from the lentils, as well as vitamins and minerals from the mixed vegetables. The whole wheat bread adds complex carbohydrates and fiber, which can help to fuel the body before a game. You can also add other vegetables to the soup, such as bell peppers or mushrooms, to increase the nutrient content.

Recipe: Grilled Tofu with Mixed Vegetables and Brown Rice:

Ingredients:

- 1 block firm tofu, drained and sliced
- 1 red bell pepper, sliced
- 1 yellow bell pepper, sliced
- 1 zucchini, sliced
- 1 onion, sliced
- 2 tablespoons olive oil
- 2 tablespoons soy sauce
- 2 cloves garlic, minced
- 1 teaspoon paprika
- Salt and pepper, to taste
- 1 cup brown rice
- 2 cups water

Instructions:

1. Preheat grill to medium-high heat.
2. In a bowl, mix together the olive oil, soy sauce, minced garlic, paprika, salt, and pepper.
3. Add the sliced tofu to the marinade and let sit for 10-15 minutes.
4. In a pot, bring 2 cups of water to a boil. Add the brown rice, cover, and reduce heat to low. Let simmer for 40-45 minutes, or until the rice is tender.

5. While the rice is cooking, grill the marinated tofu slices for 2-3 minutes on each side, or until grill marks appear.

6. In a separate pan, sauté the sliced bell peppers, zucchini, and onion with a little bit of olive oil until tender.

7. Serve the grilled tofu with the sautéed vegetables and a side of brown rice.

This recipe is a great source of plant-based protein from the tofu and complex carbohydrates from the brown rice. The mixed vegetables provide vitamins, minerals, and fiber. You can also add other vegetables to the dish, such as broccoli or mushrooms, to increase the nutrient content.

Recipe: Broiled White Fish with Mixed Vegetables and Roasted Red Potatoes:

Ingredients:

- 4 white fish fillets, such as tilapia or cod
- 2 red bell peppers, sliced
- 1 yellow squash, sliced
- 1 zucchini, sliced
- 1 onion, sliced
- 1 tablespoon olive oil
- Salt and pepper, to taste
- 4 red potatoes, cubed
- 2 tablespoons olive oil

- 1 teaspoon dried rosemary
- Salt and pepper, to taste

Instructions:

1. Preheat broiler to high.
2. Place the white fish fillets on a baking sheet lined with aluminum foil. Season with salt and pepper.
3. In a bowl, mix together the sliced red bell peppers, yellow squash, zucchini, onion, and olive oil. Season with salt and pepper.
4. Spread the mixed vegetables on a separate baking sheet lined with aluminum foil.
5. In another bowl, mix together the cubed red potatoes, olive oil, dried rosemary, salt, and pepper.
6. Spread the red potato mixture on a third baking sheet lined with aluminum foil.
7. Place all three baking sheets in the oven and broil for 8-10 minutes, or until the fish is cooked through and the vegetables and potatoes are tender and golden brown.
8. Serve the broiled white fish with the mixed vegetables and roasted red potatoes.

This recipe is a great source of protein and healthy fats from the white fish, as well as complex carbohydrates from the red potatoes. The mixed vegetables provide vitamins, minerals, and fiber. You can also use different types of vegetables or fish, such as salmon or halibut, depending on your preference.

CHAPTER 3:
BEST FOODS RIGHT BEFORE A GAME

As a soccer player, what you eat before a game can have a significant impact on your performance. Eating the right foods can provide your body with the energy it needs to perform at its best, while also reducing the risk of fatigue and injury. Here are some of the best foods to eat before a soccer game:

> **Complex Carbohydrates:** Complex carbohydrates are an excellent source of energy for soccer players. They are broken down slowly by the body, providing a steady supply of energy throughout the game. Some good sources of complex carbohydrates include whole grain bread, brown rice, pasta, and sweet potatoes.
>
> **Lean Protein:** Lean protein is essential for building and repairing muscle tissue. It also helps keep you feeling full and satisfied, which can prevent overeating before a game. Good sources of lean protein include chicken, turkey, fish, eggs, and low-fat dairy products.
>
> **Fruits and Vegetables:** Fruits and vegetables are an excellent source of vitamins, minerals, and antioxidants, which can help improve overall health and reduce the risk of injury. They are also low in calories and high in fiber,

which can help you feel full and satisfied without consuming too many calories. Some good options include bananas, berries, oranges, leafy greens, and broccoli.

Nuts and Seeds: Nuts and seeds are a great source of healthy fats and protein, which can help keep you feeling full and satisfied. They also contain important nutrients like magnesium, which can help reduce muscle cramps and improve overall performance. Good options include almonds, cashews, pumpkin seeds, and chia seeds.

Water: Staying hydrated is crucial for soccer players, especially before a game. Drinking water can help regulate body temperature, improve mental focus, and prevent dehydration, which can lead to fatigue and muscle cramps. Aim to drink at least 16-20 ounces of water 2-3 hours before the game, and then sip on water throughout the game.

In conclusion, eating the right foods before a soccer game can help improve performance, reduce the risk of injury, and keep you feeling energized throughout the game. Incorporating complex carbohydrates, lean protein, fruits and vegetables, nuts and seeds, and plenty of water into your pre-game meal can help ensure that you are adequately fueled and ready to perform at your best on the field.

10 Recipes for a Soccer Player to Eat Right Before a Game:

1. Banana and Peanut Butter Toast: Toast a slice of whole grain bread, spread a tablespoon of natural peanut butter, and top with sliced bananas.

2. Greek Yogurt with Fruit and Nuts: Mix plain Greek yogurt with sliced fruit, such as berries or mango, and sprinkle with nuts or granola for added crunch.

3. Oatmeal with Fruit and Almonds: Cook oats with water or milk, top with sliced fruit, such as apples or peaches, and sprinkle with almonds or walnuts.

4. Whole Wheat Turkey Sandwich: Spread mustard or hummus on whole wheat bread and add turkey breast, lettuce, tomato, and avocado.

5. Whole Wheat Bagel with Cream Cheese and Smoked Salmon: Toast a whole wheat bagel, spread with cream cheese, and top with smoked salmon and sliced tomatoes.

6. Turkey and Cheese Wrap: Spread mustard on a whole wheat tortilla, top with sliced turkey, cheese, lettuce, and tomato. Roll up and cut into bite-sized pieces.

7. Grilled Chicken and Vegetable Skewers: Skewer chicken, cherry tomatoes, bell peppers, and onion, and grill until cooked through.

8. Brown Rice and Grilled Shrimp Bowl: Cook brown rice, top with grilled shrimp, mixed vegetables, and a squeeze of lemon juice.

9. Grilled Shrimp Tacos: Grill shrimp with chili powder and lime juice, then serve on whole wheat tortillas with shredded cabbage and salsa.

10. Hard Boiled Eggs and Fruit: Slice hard boiled eggs and serve with sliced fruit, such as oranges or kiwi, for a quick and easy snack.

Remember to eat these meals at least 2-3 hours before the game to give your body enough time to digest and avoid any discomfort during the game.

Recipe: Banana and Peanut Butter Toast

Ingredients:

- 2 slices of whole wheat bread
- 1 ripe banana, sliced
- 2 tablespoons of natural peanut butter
- 1 teaspoon of honey (optional)

Instructions:

1. Toast the slices of whole wheat bread in a toaster until they are lightly browned.
2. Spread the peanut butter evenly over each slice of toast.
3. Place the sliced banana on top of the peanut butter.
4. Drizzle with honey, if desired.
5. Serve immediately and enjoy!

This recipe is quick, easy, and provides a good balance of carbohydrates, protein, and healthy fats to fuel your body before a soccer game. The banana provides natural sugars for quick energy, while the peanut butter adds protein and healthy fats for sustained energy. The whole wheat bread provides complex carbohydrates for long-lasting energy, and the honey adds a touch of sweetness without causing a sugar crash.

Recipe: Greek Yogurt with Fruits and Nuts

Ingredients:

- 1 cup of plain Greek yogurt
- 1/2 cup of mixed berries (such as strawberries, blueberries, and raspberries)

- 1/4 cup of chopped nuts (such as almonds or walnuts)
- 1 teaspoon of honey (optional)

Instructions:

1. Scoop the Greek yogurt into a bowl.
2. Wash the mixed berries and slice any larger fruits into bite-sized pieces. Add the fruit to the bowl with the Greek yogurt.
3. Sprinkle the chopped nuts over the top of the yogurt and fruit.
4. Drizzle with honey, if desired.
5. Serve immediately and enjoy!

This recipe is a great choice for a pre-soccer game meal or snack, as it provides a good balance of protein, healthy fats, and carbohydrates. Greek yogurt is a good source of protein, while the mixed berries provide natural sugars and vitamins. The nuts add healthy fats and crunch, and the honey adds a touch of sweetness without causing a sugar crash.

Recipe: Oatmeal with Fruit and Almonds

Ingredients:

- 1/2 cup of rolled oats
- 1 cup of water or milk (almond milk or other milk alternatives can be used)
- 1/2 cup of mixed berries (such as strawberries, blueberries, and raspberries)
- 1/4 cup of chopped almonds

- 1 teaspoon of honey (optional)

Instructions:

1. Combine the rolled oats and water or milk in a small saucepan.
2. Cook over medium heat, stirring occasionally, until the oats are tender and the mixture has thickened.
3. Wash the mixed berries and slice any larger fruits into bite-sized pieces. Add the fruit to the oatmeal.
4. Sprinkle the chopped almonds over the top of the oatmeal and fruit.
5. Drizzle with honey, if desired.
6. Serve immediately and enjoy!

This recipe is a great choice for a pre-soccer game breakfast, as it provides complex carbohydrates, protein, and healthy fats to fuel your body. The oatmeal is a good source of complex carbohydrates, which provide sustained energy, while the mixed berries provide natural sugars and vitamins. The almonds add healthy fats and crunch, and the honey adds a touch of sweetness without causing a sugar crash.

Recipe: Whole Wheat Turkey Sandwich

Ingredients:

- 2 slices of whole wheat bread
- 3 ounces of sliced turkey breast
- 1 tablespoon of mustard
- 1 tablespoon of hummus
- 1/2 cup of baby spinach or lettuce leaves

- Optional: sliced tomato and avocado

Instructions:

1. Toast the slices of whole wheat bread.
2. Spread mustard on one slice of bread and hummus on the other slice.
3. Layer the sliced turkey on top of the mustard and top with baby spinach or lettuce leaves.
4. Add optional sliced tomato and avocado if desired.
5. Top with the other slice of bread and slice the sandwich in half.
6. Serve immediately and enjoy!

This recipe is a great choice for a pre-soccer game meal or snack, as it provides a good balance of carbohydrates, protein, and healthy fats. The whole wheat bread provides complex carbohydrates, while the turkey is a good source of protein. The hummus and avocado (if added) add healthy fats and additional protein. The mustard adds a zesty flavor without added sugars or calories.

Recipe: Whole Wheat Bagel with Cream Cheese and Smoked Salmon

Ingredients:

- 1 whole wheat bagel
- 2 tablespoons of cream cheese
- 2 ounces of smoked salmon
- Sliced red onion

- Capers
- Fresh dill

Instructions:

1. Slice the whole wheat bagel in half and toast it.
2. Spread cream cheese on both halves of the bagel.
3. Top one half of the bagel with smoked salmon.
4. Add sliced red onion and capers to the top of the salmon.
5. Sprinkle fresh dill on top of the salmon and other toppings.
6. Top with the other half of the bagel and slice in half.
7. Serve immediately and enjoy!

This recipe is a great choice for a pre-soccer game breakfast or lunch, as it provides a good balance of carbohydrates, protein, and healthy fats. The whole wheat bagel provides complex carbohydrates, while the smoked salmon is a good source of protein and healthy omega-3 fatty acids. The cream cheese adds a touch of creaminess and a bit of protein. The red onion and capers provide additional flavor and texture, and the dill adds freshness and flavor.

Recipe: Turkey and Cheese Wrap

Ingredients:

- 1 whole wheat wrap
- 3 ounces of sliced turkey breast
- 1 slice of cheese

- 1/4 avocado, sliced
- 1/4 cup of shredded lettuce or baby spinach
- 1 tablespoon of hummus or mustard

Instructions:

1. Lay the whole wheat wrap flat on a plate or cutting board.
2. Spread hummus or mustard on the wrap.
3. Layer the sliced turkey, cheese, sliced avocado, and shredded lettuce or spinach on top of the wrap.
4. Roll the wrap tightly, tucking in the sides as you go.
5. Cut the wrap in half and serve immediately.

This recipe is a great choice for a pre-soccer game meal or snack, as it provides a good balance of carbohydrates, protein, and healthy fats. The whole wheat wrap provides complex carbohydrates, while the turkey is a good source of protein. The cheese and avocado add healthy fats and additional protein. The lettuce or spinach provides fiber and other important nutrients. The hummus or mustard adds a touch of flavor without added sugars or calories.

Recipe: Grilled Chicken and Vegetable Skewers

Ingredients:

- 2 boneless, skinless chicken breasts, cut into chunks
- 1 red bell pepper, cut into chunks
- 1 yellow bell pepper, cut into chunks
- 1 zucchini, sliced into rounds

- 1 red onion, cut into chunks
- 1 tablespoon of olive oil
- Salt and pepper, to taste

Instructions:

1. Soak wooden skewers in water for at least 30 minutes.
2. Preheat grill or grill pan to medium-high heat.
3. Thread the chicken and vegetables onto skewers, alternating chicken and vegetables.
4. Brush the skewers with olive oil and season with salt and pepper.
5. Grill the skewers for 8-10 minutes, turning occasionally, until chicken is cooked through and vegetables are slightly charred.
6. Serve immediately.

This recipe is a great choice for a pre-soccer game dinner, as it provides a good balance of carbohydrates, protein, and healthy fats. The chicken is a good source of protein, while the vegetables provide important nutrients and fiber. The olive oil adds healthy fats and flavor without added sugars or calories.

Recipe: Brown Rice and Grilled Shrimp Bowl

Ingredients:

- 1 cup of brown rice
- 1 pound of raw shrimp, peeled and deveined
- 1 tablespoon of olive oil

- Salt and pepper, to taste
- 1 avocado, diced
- 1 cucumber, diced
- 1 bell pepper, diced
- 1 carrot, grated
- 2 tablespoons of chopped cilantro
- 1 lime, cut into wedges

Instructions:

1. Cook brown rice according to package instructions.
2. Preheat grill or grill pan to medium-high heat.
3. Thread the shrimp onto skewers and brush with olive oil. Season with salt and pepper.
4. Grill the shrimp for 2-3 minutes per side, until pink and slightly charred.
5. In a bowl, add cooked brown rice, diced avocado, cucumber, bell pepper, and grated carrot.
6. Top with grilled shrimp and chopped cilantro.
7. Squeeze lime wedges over the bowl before serving.

This recipe is a nutritious and tasty option for a pre-soccer game meal. Brown rice provides complex carbohydrates, while shrimp is a great source of lean protein. The vegetables and avocado add important vitamins, minerals, and healthy fats. The cilantro and lime juice provide a fresh and zesty flavor without added sugars or calories.

Recipe: Grilled Shrimp Tacos

Ingredients:

- 1 pound of raw shrimp, peeled and deveined
- 2 tablespoons of olive oil
- 1 tablespoon of chili powder
- 1/2 teaspoon of garlic powder
- 1/2 teaspoon of cumin
- Salt and pepper, to taste
- 8 small corn tortillas
- 2 cups of shredded cabbage
- 1 avocado, diced
- 1/2 cup of chopped cilantro
- 1 lime, cut into wedges

Instructions:

1. Preheat grill or grill pan to medium-high heat.
2. In a bowl, mix together olive oil, chili powder, garlic powder, cumin, salt, and pepper.
3. Add the shrimp to the bowl and toss until evenly coated in the spice mixture.
4. Grill the shrimp for 2-3 minutes per side, until pink and slightly charred.
5. Warm the corn tortillas on the grill for 30 seconds on each side.
6. Assemble the tacos by adding shredded cabbage, grilled

shrimp, diced avocado, and chopped cilantro to each tortilla.

7. Squeeze lime wedges over the tacos before serving.

This recipe is a flavorful and satisfying option for a pre-soccer game meal. Shrimp is a great source of lean protein, while the spices provide a boost of flavor without added calories. The cabbage and avocado add important vitamins, minerals, and healthy fats. The tortillas provide a source of carbohydrates for energy.

Recipe: Hard Boiled Eggs and Fruit

Ingredients:

- 4 hard boiled eggs
- 1 apple, sliced
- 1 cup of mixed berries (such as blueberries, raspberries, and strawberries)
- 1 tablespoon of honey (optional)

Instructions:

1. Prepare the hard boiled eggs according to your preferred method. Once cooked, peel the eggs and set aside.
2. Wash and slice the apple.
3. Wash and prepare the mixed berries.
4. Arrange the hard boiled eggs, apple slices, and mixed berries on a plate.
5. Drizzle honey over the fruit, if desired.

This recipe is a simple and convenient option for a pre-soccer game meal. Hard boiled eggs are a great source of protein, while the fruit provides important vitamins, minerals, and carbohydrates for energy. The honey adds a touch of sweetness and can help boost energy levels. It's also a great option for those who may not have a lot of time to prepare a meal or prefer something light before exercising.

CHAPTER 4:
BEST FOODS DURING A GAME

During a soccer game, it's important to consume foods that can help maintain energy levels, hydration, and endurance. Here are some examples of foods that are commonly recommended to eat during a soccer game:

Sports drinks: Sports drinks can help to replenish electrolytes and carbohydrates lost through sweat during exercise. They can also help to maintain hydration levels, which is crucial during a soccer game.

Energy gels: Energy gels are a quick and easy source of carbohydrates that can help to maintain energy levels during a soccer game. They are designed to be consumed quickly and easily, without the need for chewing.

Bananas: Bananas are a great source of carbohydrates and potassium, which can help to maintain energy levels and prevent muscle cramps. They are also easy to digest and can be carried around in a backpack during the game.

Energy bars: Energy bars can provide a quick source of carbohydrates, protein, and healthy fats during a soccer game. Look for bars that are high in complex carbohydrates and low in sugar.

Sandwiches: Sandwiches made with whole grain bread, lean protein, and vegetables can provide a balanced source of nutrients during a soccer game. They are also easy to carry around and can be customized to individual preferences.

It's important to note that the specific foods that are best to eat during a soccer game may vary depending on individual preferences, dietary restrictions, and the length of the game. It's also important to stay hydrated during the game by drinking water or sports drinks regularly.

Sports Drinks

Sports drinks are a popular choice for soccer players because they can help replenish fluids and electrolytes lost through sweat during intense exercise. Here are some of the best sports drinks for soccer players:

Gatorade: Gatorade is one of the most well-known sports drinks and is often used by soccer players. It contains a mix of carbohydrates and electrolytes to help replenish energy stores and prevent dehydration.

Powerade: Powerade is another popular sports drink that contains a mix of carbohydrates and electrolytes. It also contains vitamins B3, B6, and B12, which can help boost energy levels.

BodyArmor: BodyArmor is a newer sports drink that contains coconut water and electrolytes for hydration, as well as vitamins and antioxidants for added health benefits.

NUUN Sport: NUUN Sport is a tablet that dissolves in water to create a sports drink. It contains electrolytes and a small amount of carbohydrates for energy, but is lower in sugar than many other sports drinks.

Skratch Labs Hydration Mix: Skratch Labs Hydration Mix is another powder that can be added to water to create a sports drink. It contains electrolytes and carbohydrates from real fruit for sustained energy.

It's important to note that while sports drinks can be helpful for soccer players, they should not be used as a replacement for water. Drinking plenty of water before, during, and after games is still the best way to stay hydrated.

Energy Gels

Energy gels are a popular choice for soccer players because they can quickly provide a boost of energy during a game or training session. Here are some of the best energy gels for soccer players:

GU Energy Gel: GU Energy Gel is a popular choice among endurance athletes, including soccer players. It contains a blend of carbohydrates and amino acids to provide a quick energy boost and help delay fatigue.

Clif Shot Energy Gel: Clif Shot Energy Gel is another popular energy gel that contains a mix of carbohydrates and electrolytes. It also contains caffeine to help boost energy levels and improve focus.

PowerBar PowerGel: PowerBar PowerGel is a gel that contains a mix of carbohydrates and electrolytes for energy and hydration. It also contains sodium and potassium to help maintain electrolyte balance.

Honey Stinger Energy Gel: Honey Stinger Energy Gel is made with organic honey and contains a mix of carbohydrates and electrolytes. It also contains B vitamins to help convert food into energy.

Science in Sport Energy Gel: Science in Sport Energy Gel is a gel that contains a blend of carbohydrates, electrolytes, and caffeine for energy and focus. It's designed to be easy to digest and can be taken without water.

It's important to note that energy gels should be used in moderation and should be consumed with water to prevent dehydration. It's also a good idea to test energy gels during practice before using them during a game to ensure that they don't cause any digestive issues.

Bananas

Bananas are a great snack for soccer players because they're easy to digest, provide quick energy, and are packed with nutrients like potassium. Here are some of the best ways to eat bananas during a soccer game:

Fresh banana: One of the easiest ways to eat a banana during a soccer game is to simply peel it and eat it as is. This is a quick and convenient option that requires no preparation.

Banana slices: If you prefer, you can slice a banana into small pieces before the game and store them in a container. This makes them easier to eat quickly and can also help prevent any digestive issues.

Banana smoothie: Another option is to blend a banana with some water or milk to create a quick and easy banana smoothie. This can be stored in a thermos and sipped throughout the game to provide sustained energy.

Peanut butter and banana sandwich: For a more substantial snack, you can make a peanut butter and banana sandwich on whole wheat bread. This provides a mix of carbohydrates and protein to help sustain energy levels.

Banana and yogurt: Another option is to mix sliced banana with some plain yogurt and a drizzle of honey for a quick and easy snack that's packed with nutrients.

Remember to consume bananas in moderation and in conjunction with other snacks to ensure a balanced diet during a soccer game.

Energy Bars

Choosing the right energy bars during a soccer game is important to maintain energy levels and prevent fatigue. Here are some of the best energy bars to eat during a soccer game:

Clif Bar: Clif Bars are a popular option for athletes because they are made with wholesome ingredients like organic rolled oats, organic dates, and organic almond butter. They come in a variety of flavors and provide a balance of carbohydrates, protein, and fat.

KIND Bars: KIND Bars are made with simple ingredients like nuts, dried fruit, and honey. They are gluten-free and provide a good balance of protein and healthy fats.

Larabar: Larabars are made with just a few simple ingredients like dates, nuts, and fruit. They are gluten-free, dairy-free, and provide a good source of fiber and natural sugars.

RXBAR: RXBARs are made with whole food ingredients like egg whites, nuts, and dates. They are gluten-free, dairy-free, and provide a good source of protein.

ProBar: ProBars are made with organic, non-GMO ingredients like oats, nuts, and seeds. They come in a variety of flavors and provide a good balance of carbohydrates, protein, and fat.

When choosing an energy bar, it's important to read the label and choose a bar that is low in added sugars and artificial ingredients. Additionally, it's important to consume energy bars in moderation and in conjunction with other snacks to ensure a balanced diet during a soccer game.

Sandwiches

Sandwiches can be a convenient and tasty option for soccer players during a game. Here are some of the best sandwiches to eat during a soccer game:

Turkey and avocado sandwich: Use whole wheat bread and add sliced turkey, avocado, lettuce, tomato, and a spread of hummus or mustard for a satisfying and protein-packed sandwich.

Grilled chicken sandwich: Grill or bake a chicken breast and place it on whole wheat bread with lettuce, tomato, and a low-fat cheese for a filling and protein-rich sandwich.

Peanut butter and jelly sandwich: A classic sandwich that can provide quick energy, use whole wheat bread and natural peanut butter for a healthier option.

Veggie sandwich: Load up whole wheat bread with sliced cucumbers, bell peppers, lettuce, tomato, avocado, and a hummus or mustard spread for a fiber-packed and nutrient-dense sandwich.

Tuna sandwich: Use canned tuna in water, mix it with light mayo or Greek yogurt, add sliced tomato, lettuce, and whole wheat bread for a protein-rich sandwich.

Roast beef and cheese sandwich: Use lean roast beef and a low-fat cheese on whole wheat bread with lettuce and tomato for a satisfying and protein-packed sandwich.

Egg salad sandwich: Make egg salad with Greek yogurt or light mayo, add lettuce and tomato, and place it on whole wheat bread for a protein and fiber-rich sandwich.

It's important to note that sandwiches should be consumed in moderation during a game to prevent indigestion or stomach discomfort.

CHAPTER 5:
BEST FOODS AFTER A GAME

After a soccer game, it's important to refuel your body with the right nutrients to support recovery and help you feel energized for your next training session or game. Here are some of the best foods to eat after a soccer game:

Lean protein: Eating lean protein, such as chicken, fish, tofu, or beans, can help to support muscle growth and repair. Protein is essential for repairing the muscle damage that can occur during intense exercise like soccer.

Whole grains: Whole grains, such as quinoa, brown rice, or whole wheat bread, can help to replenish glycogen stores in the muscles. Glycogen is the primary source of energy used during exercise, and replenishing it after a game can help to support recovery and refuel for the next game.

Vegetables: Vegetables are an important source of vitamins, minerals, and fiber, which can help to support overall health and well-being. Eating a variety of colorful vegetables can help to provide important nutrients for recovery.

Fruits: Fruits are a great source of carbohydrates and can help to replenish energy stores after a game. They are also high in vitamins and minerals, which can help to support recovery and overall health.

Water: Rehydration is an important part of recovery after a soccer game. Drinking plenty of water can help to replace fluids lost through sweat during the game and support overall health.

Healthy fats: Healthy fats, such as those found in avocados, nuts, or olive oil, can help to support brain function and overall health. They can also help to keep you feeling full and satisfied after a game.

It's important to avoid consuming too much processed food, sugar, or alcohol after a game, as these can have a negative impact on recovery and overall health. Eating a balanced meal with a combination of protein, carbohydrates, and healthy fats can help to support recovery and prepare you for your next game or training session.

10 recipes for a soccer player after the match:

1. Grilled turkey burger, roasted sweet potato wedges and a side salad with mixed greens
2. Quinoa and black bean salad with roasted vegetables and a lemon vinaigrette
3. Grilled salmon with roasted sweet potatoes and steamed asparagus
4. Whole wheat pita with hummus, grilled chicken, and mixed vegetables
5. Grilled flank steak with roasted root vegetables and sautéed spinach
6. Tuna and mixed vegetable salad with a citrus vinaigrette dressing

7. Brown rice bowl with grilled tofu, mixed vegetables, and a peanut sauce
8. Baked sweet potato with black beans, salsa, and Greek yogurt
9. Turkey and vegetable stir-fry with brown rice
10. Grilled shrimp skewers with mixed vegetables and a quinoa salad

Remember to prioritize protein, complex carbohydrates, and plenty of fruits and vegetables to help replenish your energy stores and aid in muscle recovery.

Recipe: Grilled Turkey Burger, Roasted Sweet Potato Wedges and a Side Salad with Mixed Greens

For the turkey burger:
- 1 lb ground turkey
- 1/4 cup breadcrumbs
- 1/4 cup diced onion
- 1/4 cup diced green pepper
- 1 garlic clove, minced
- 1 tsp Worcestershire sauce
- 1 egg
- Salt and pepper to taste

For the sweet potato wedges:
- 2 sweet potatoes, cut into wedges
- 2 tbsp olive oil
- 1 tsp paprika

- 1 tsp garlic powder
- Salt and pepper to taste

For the side salad:

- 4 cups mixed greens
- 1 cup cherry tomatoes, halved
- 1/2 cucumber, sliced
- 1/4 red onion, thinly sliced
- 1/4 cup crumbled feta cheese
- 2 tbsp balsamic vinegar
- 2 tbsp olive oil
- Salt and pepper to taste

Instructions:

1. Preheat grill to medium-high heat.
2. In a large mixing bowl, combine ground turkey, breadcrumbs, diced onion, diced green pepper, minced garlic, Worcestershire sauce, egg, salt, and pepper. Mix well.
3. Form the mixture into four patties.
4. In a separate mixing bowl, toss the sweet potato wedges with olive oil, paprika, garlic powder, salt, and pepper.
5. Place the turkey burgers and sweet potato wedges on the grill. Cook for about 5-6 minutes per side, or until the burgers are cooked through and the sweet potatoes are tender and crispy.

6. While the burgers and sweet potatoes are cooking, prepare the side salad. In a large mixing bowl, combine the mixed greens, cherry tomatoes, cucumber, red onion, and feta cheese.

7. In a small mixing bowl, whisk together the balsamic vinegar, olive oil, salt, and pepper to make the dressing.

8. Once the burgers and sweet potatoes are done, serve them hot with the side salad on the side. Drizzle the salad with the dressing and enjoy!

Recipe: Quinoa and Black Bean Salad with Roasted Vegetables and a Lemon Vinaigrette

Ingredients:

- 1 cup quinoa
- 1 can black beans, drained and rinsed
- 1 red bell pepper, chopped
- 1 yellow bell pepper, chopped
- 1 zucchini, chopped
- 1 red onion, chopped
- 2 tbsp olive oil
- 1 tsp cumin
- 1 tsp chili powder
- Salt and pepper to taste
- Juice of 1 lemon
- 2 tbsp olive oil

- 1 tbsp honey
- 1 clove garlic, minced
- Salt and pepper to taste
- Fresh cilantro, chopped

Instructions:

1. Cook quinoa according to package instructions and set aside.
2. Preheat oven to 400°F.
3. In a bowl, mix chopped red and yellow bell peppers, zucchini, and red onion with 2 tbsp of olive oil, cumin, chili powder, salt, and pepper.
4. Spread vegetables onto a baking sheet and roast in the preheated oven for 15-20 minutes, until tender.
5. In a separate bowl, whisk together lemon juice, 2 tbsp of olive oil, honey, garlic, salt, and pepper to make the vinaigrette.
6. In a large bowl, mix cooked quinoa, roasted vegetables, and black beans.
7. Pour the vinaigrette over the quinoa salad and toss to coat.
8. Garnish with fresh cilantro and serve.

This quinoa and black bean salad is packed with protein and fiber, which are important for muscle recovery after a soccer match. The roasted vegetables add a delicious flavor and texture to the salad, while the lemon vinaigrette gives it a tangy and refreshing taste. It's a perfect post-match meal to refuel and replenish your body.

Recipe: Grilled Salmon with Roasted Sweet Potatoes and Steamed Asparagus

Grilled Salmon with Roasted Sweet Potatoes and Steamed Asparagus Recipe:

Ingredients:

- 4 salmon fillets
- 2 large sweet potatoes, cut into wedges
- 1 bunch asparagus, trimmed
- 2 tbsp olive oil
- 2 garlic cloves, minced
- Salt and pepper
- Lemon wedges, for serving

Instructions:

1. Preheat the oven to 400°F (200°C). Line a baking sheet with parchment paper.
2. In a small bowl, mix together the olive oil, minced garlic, salt, and pepper.
3. Toss the sweet potato wedges with half of the olive oil mixture and spread them out on the prepared baking sheet. Roast for 20-25 minutes, or until tender and lightly browned.
4. Meanwhile, preheat a grill or grill pan over medium-high heat. Brush the salmon fillets with the remaining olive oil mixture and season with salt and pepper.
5. Grill the salmon fillets for 3-4 minutes per side, or until

cooked to your desired level of doneness.

6. While the salmon and sweet potatoes are cooking, steam the asparagus for 3-4 minutes, or until tender-crisp.

7. Serve the grilled salmon with the roasted sweet potatoes, steamed asparagus, and lemon wedges on the side.

Recipe: Whole Wheat Pita with Hummus, Grilled Chicken, and Mixed Vegetables

Ingredients:

- 1 whole wheat pita
- 1/4 cup of hummus
- 4 oz. of grilled chicken breast, sliced
- 1/4 cup of mixed vegetables (sliced cucumbers, tomatoes, red onions, etc.)
- Salt and pepper, to taste

Instructions:

1. Preheat grill or grill pan to medium-high heat.
2. Grill chicken breast for 5-7 minutes on each side or until cooked through.
3. Cut the pita in half and spread hummus evenly on both sides.
4. Add the grilled chicken slices to one side of the pita and the mixed vegetables to the other side.
5. Sprinkle with salt and pepper to taste.
6. Serve and enjoy!

Optional: You can add additional toppings like lettuce, avocado, or feta cheese for extra flavor and nutrition.

Recipe: Grilled Flank Steak with Roasted Root Vegetables and Sautéed Spinach:

Ingredients:

- 1 lb. flank steak
- 1 tsp. olive oil
- 1 tsp. kosher salt
- 1/2 tsp. black pepper
- 1 lb. mixed root vegetables (carrots, parsnips, turnips, beets), peeled and chopped into 1-inch pieces
- 2 cloves garlic, minced
- 1 tsp. dried rosemary
- 2 tbsp. olive oil
- 5 oz. baby spinach

Instructions:

1. Preheat grill to high heat. Rub steak with 1 tsp. olive oil and sprinkle with salt and pepper.
2. Grill steak for 4-6 minutes per side, or until desired doneness is reached. Let rest for 5-10 minutes before slicing.
3. Preheat oven to 400°F. Toss mixed root vegetables with minced garlic, dried rosemary, 2 tbsp. olive oil, and a pinch of salt and pepper.
4. Spread vegetables out in a single layer on a baking sheet and roast for 25-30 minutes, or until tender and golden

brown.

5. While vegetables are roasting, sauté baby spinach in a non-stick pan over medium heat until wilted.
6. Serve sliced steak with roasted root vegetables and sautéed spinach.

Recipe: Tuna and Mixed Vegetable Salad with a Citrus Vinaigrette Dressing

Ingredients:

- 1 can of tuna, drained
- 2 cups mixed greens
- 1 cup cherry tomatoes, halved
- 1 cup sliced cucumbers
- 1/2 cup sliced red onions
- 1/2 cup sliced carrots
- 1/4 cup chopped fresh parsley
- 1/4 cup chopped fresh cilantro
- Juice of 1 lemon
- 2 tablespoons olive oil
- Salt and pepper to taste

Instructions:

1. In a large bowl, combine the mixed greens, cherry tomatoes, sliced cucumbers, red onions, and sliced carrots.
2. Add the drained tuna to the bowl and mix well.
3. In a small bowl, whisk together the lemon juice, olive

oil, salt, and pepper.

4. Pour the dressing over the salad and toss to combine.

5. Garnish the salad with chopped fresh parsley and cilantro.

6. Serve immediately or store in the refrigerator for up to 24 hours.

Recipe: Brown Rice Bowl with Grilled Tofu, Mixed Vegetables, and a Peanut Sauce

Ingredients:

- 1 cup of brown rice
- 1 block of firm tofu
- 2 tablespoons of olive oil
- 1 tablespoon of soy sauce
- 1 teaspoon of garlic powder
- Salt and pepper
- 2 cups of mixed vegetables (such as bell peppers, broccoli, carrots, and snap peas)
- 1/4 cup of peanut butter
- 2 tablespoons of honey
- 2 tablespoons of soy sauce
- 1 tablespoon of rice vinegar
- 1 tablespoon of sesame oil
- 1 tablespoon of water

Instructions:

1. Cook the brown rice according to the package instructions and set aside.

2. Cut the tofu into cubes and marinate in 1 tablespoon of olive oil, soy sauce, garlic powder, salt, and pepper for at least 30 minutes.

3. Heat the remaining tablespoon of olive oil in a pan over medium heat. Add the mixed vegetables and sauté until tender.

4. Grill the marinated tofu on a grill or in a pan until crispy.

5. In a small bowl, whisk together the peanut butter, honey, soy sauce, rice vinegar, sesame oil, and water to make the peanut sauce.

6. Assemble the bowl by dividing the cooked brown rice, mixed vegetables, and grilled tofu among 4 bowls. Drizzle the peanut sauce over the top and serve.

Recipe: Baked Sweet Potato with Black Beans, Salsa, and Greek Yogurt

Ingredients:

- 1 large sweet potato
- 1/2 cup canned black beans, drained and rinsed
- 1/4 cup salsa
- 2 tablespoons Greek yogurt
- Salt and pepper to taste

Instructions:

1. Preheat oven to 400°F (200°C).
2. Wash sweet potato and pierce it several times with a fork. Place it on a baking sheet and bake for 45-50 minutes, or until tender.
3. Meanwhile, in a small saucepan, heat the black beans over medium heat until warmed through.
4. Once the sweet potato is done, cut it open and sprinkle with salt and pepper to taste.
5. Top the sweet potato with the warm black beans, salsa, and a dollop of Greek yogurt.
6. Serve immediately.

Optional: You can also add diced avocado or chopped cilantro on top for extra flavor and nutrition.

Recipe: Turkey and Vegetable Stir-Fry with Brown Rice

Ingredients:

- 1 lb. ground turkey
- 1 red bell pepper, sliced
- 1 green bell pepper, sliced
- 1 yellow onion, sliced
- 2 garlic cloves, minced
- 2 tbsp. olive oil
- Salt and pepper to taste
- 2 cups cooked brown rice
- 1/4 cup low-sodium soy sauce

- 1 tsp. sesame oil
- 1 tsp. honey
- 1/2 tsp. ground ginger

Instructions:

1. In a large skillet or wok, heat 1 tbsp. olive oil over medium-high heat. Add ground turkey and cook until browned and cooked through, stirring occasionally. Remove from skillet and set aside.

2. Add another 1 tbsp. of olive oil to the skillet. Add sliced bell peppers and onions, and cook for 5-7 minutes until softened. Add minced garlic and cook for another 1-2 minutes.

3. Add cooked ground turkey back to the skillet with the vegetables. Add salt and pepper to taste.

4. In a small bowl, whisk together low-sodium soy sauce, sesame oil, honey, and ground ginger. Pour over the turkey and vegetable mixture and stir to combine.

5. Serve turkey and vegetable stir-fry over cooked brown rice.

Recipe: Grilled Shrimp Skewers with Quinoa Salad

Ingredients:

- 1 pound large shrimp, peeled and deveined
- 1 red bell pepper, seeded and cut into chunks
- 1 green bell pepper, seeded and cut into chunks
- 1 small red onion, cut into chunks
- 1 tablespoon olive oil

- 1 teaspoon garlic powder
- Salt and pepper to taste
- 1 cup quinoa, rinsed
- 2 cups water or low-sodium chicken broth
- 1/4 cup chopped fresh parsley
- 2 tablespoons chopped fresh mint
- 2 tablespoons chopped fresh basil
- 1/4 cup chopped cucumber
- 1/4 cup chopped tomato
- 1/4 cup chopped red onion
- 2 tablespoons olive oil
- 2 tablespoons fresh lemon juice
- Salt and pepper to taste

Instructions:

1. Preheat grill to medium-high heat.
2. Thread shrimp, bell peppers, and red onion onto skewers. Brush with olive oil and sprinkle with garlic powder, salt, and pepper.
3. Grill skewers for 2-3 minutes on each side, or until shrimp is cooked through.
4. Meanwhile, bring quinoa and water or chicken broth to a boil in a medium saucepan. Reduce heat to low, cover, and simmer for 15-20 minutes, or until all the liquid is absorbed.

5. In a large bowl, combine cooked quinoa, parsley, mint, basil, cucumber, tomato, and red onion.

6. Whisk together olive oil and lemon juice in a small bowl. Pour dressing over quinoa salad and toss to coat.

7. Serve grilled shrimp skewers with quinoa salad on the side.

CHAPTER 6:
SNACKS

In addition to meals, snacks can play an important role in fueling soccer players and helping them stay fit. Snacks can provide a quick energy boost before or during a game, and can also help replenish energy and nutrients after exercise.

10 Snack Ideas for Soccer Players:

1. Fruit and nut butter: Slice up an apple or banana and pair it with a tablespoon of almond or peanut butter for a satisfying snack that provides a mix of carbohydrates, healthy fats, and protein.

2. Greek yogurt and berries: Top a cup of plain Greek yogurt with fresh berries for a snack that provides protein and carbohydrates, as well as vitamins and minerals.

3. Hard-boiled eggs: Eggs are a great source of protein and can be boiled in advance for an easy snack option. Sprinkle with a little salt and pepper for flavor.

4. Trail mix: Combine nuts, seeds, and dried fruit for a snack that provides healthy fats, protein, and carbohydrates.

5. Hummus and vegetables: Dip sliced carrots, cucumbers, and bell peppers in hummus for a snack that provides

fiber, vitamins, and minerals.

6. Rice cakes with avocado and turkey: Top a rice cake with mashed avocado and sliced turkey for a snack that provides carbohydrates, healthy fats, and protein.

7. Smoothie: Blend together milk or yogurt with frozen fruit and a scoop of protein powder for a quick and easy snack that provides carbohydrates and protein.

8. Cottage cheese and fruit: Top a serving of cottage cheese with fresh berries or sliced peaches for a snack that provides protein and carbohydrates.

9. Energy balls: Combine dates, nuts, and seeds in a food processor and roll into balls for a snack that provides healthy fats, protein, and carbohydrates.

10. Roasted chickpeas: Toss canned chickpeas with olive oil and spices and roast in the oven for a crunchy snack that provides fiber, protein, and carbohydrates.

By choosing healthy and nutrient-dense snacks, soccer players can fuel their bodies properly and support their performance on the field.

Recipe: Fruit and Nut Butter

Ingredients:

- 2 cups of mixed nuts (such as almonds, cashews, and peanuts)
- 1 tablespoon of honey (optional)
- 1 teaspoon of cinnamon (optional)
- 1 cup of chopped dried fruit (such as apricots, dates, and raisins)

- Salt to taste

Instructions:

1. Preheat your oven to 350°F (180°C).

2. Spread the mixed nuts evenly on a baking sheet and roast for 10-15 minutes or until lightly golden and fragrant.

3. Transfer the roasted nuts to a food processor and process for several minutes until the nuts form a smooth paste. You may need to stop and scrape down the sides of the processor a few times.

4. Add the honey, cinnamon, and salt (if using) to the nut butter and pulse a few times to combine.

5. Add the chopped dried fruit to the nut butter and pulse until well combined.

6. Store the fruit and nut butter in an airtight container in the refrigerator for up to two weeks.

Serve with sliced fruit or whole-grain crackers for a healthy snack that's packed with protein, fiber, and healthy fats.

Recipe: Greek Yogurt and Berries

Ingredients:

- 1 cup of Greek yogurt
- 1/2 cup of mixed berries (such as strawberries, blueberries, raspberries)

Instructions:

1. Wash the berries and slice any larger fruits into smaller

pieces.

2. Spoon the Greek yogurt into a bowl or cup.
3. Top the yogurt with the mixed berries.
4. Mix the berries and yogurt together.
5. Enjoy as a healthy snack or breakfast.

Optional: You can also add a drizzle of honey or a sprinkle of granola for added sweetness and texture.

Recipe: Hard-Boiled Eggs

Ingredients:

- Eggs
- Water

Instructions:

1. Place eggs in a single layer at the bottom of a saucepan.
2. Fill the saucepan with enough water to cover the eggs by about an inch.
3. Place the saucepan on the stove and bring the water to a rolling boil.
4. Once the water is boiling, remove the saucepan from the heat and cover with a lid.
5. Let the eggs sit in the hot water for about 9-12 minutes, depending on the size of the eggs and how well-cooked you want them.
6. After the desired cooking time, drain the hot water from the saucepan and rinse the eggs with cold water to stop

the cooking process.

7. Peel the eggs and enjoy!

You can store hard-boiled eggs in the fridge for up to one week. They make a great snack or addition to salads and sandwiches.

Recipe: Trail Mix

Ingredients:

- 1 cup raw almonds
- 1 cup raw cashews
- 1 cup raw walnuts
- 1 cup pumpkin seeds
- 1 cup sunflower seeds
- 1 cup unsweetened dried cranberries
- 1 cup unsweetened coconut flakes

Instructions:

1. Preheat the oven to 350°F (175°C).
2. Spread the almonds, cashews, walnuts, pumpkin seeds, and sunflower seeds on a baking sheet.
3. Roast the nuts and seeds in the oven for 8-10 minutes, stirring occasionally, until lightly browned and fragrant.
4. Let the nuts and seeds cool completely.
5. In a large mixing bowl, combine the roasted nuts and seeds with the dried cranberries and coconut flakes.

6. Store the trail mix in an airtight container for up to 2 weeks.

You can also customize the ingredients to your liking by adding or substituting other nuts, seeds, or dried fruits.

Recipe: Hummus and Vegetables

Ingredients:

- 1 can of chickpeas
- 1/4 cup of tahini
- 1/4 cup of lemon juice
- 2 cloves of garlic
- 1/4 cup of olive oil
- Salt and pepper to taste
- 2-3 tbsp of water, as needed
- Carrots, celery, bell peppers, or other vegetables for dipping

Instructions:

1. Drain and rinse the chickpeas and add them to a food processor.
2. Add the tahini, lemon juice, garlic, olive oil, salt, and pepper to the food processor.
3. Pulse the ingredients until they are smooth and creamy.
4. If the hummus is too thick, add water one tablespoon at a time until it reaches the desired consistency.
5. Serve the hummus with sliced vegetables for dipping.

Recipe: Rice Cakes with Avocado and Turkey

Ingredients:

- 4 rice cakes
- 1 ripe avocado, mashed
- 4 slices of deli turkey
- Salt and pepper
- Lemon juice

Instructions:

1. Toast the rice cakes until crispy.
2. Spread a generous amount of mashed avocado onto each rice cake.
3. Layer one slice of turkey on top of the avocado.
4. Season with salt, pepper, and a squeeze of lemon juice to taste.
5. Serve and enjoy!

Optional additions: You can add other vegetables such as sliced tomato, cucumber, or lettuce to the rice cakes for more flavor and nutrients.

Recipe: Smoothie

Ingredients:

- 1 banana
- 1 cup frozen mixed berries
- 1/2 cup plain Greek yogurt
- 1/2 cup unsweetened almond milk

- 1 tbsp honey (optional)
- 1 tbsp chia seeds (optional)

Instructions:

1. Peel and chop the banana into small pieces.
2. In a blender, add the chopped banana, frozen mixed berries, Greek yogurt, almond milk, and honey (if using).
3. Blend on high speed until smooth and creamy.
4. If desired, add chia seeds and pulse briefly to mix.
5. Pour into a glass and enjoy immediately.

This smoothie is packed with protein, fiber, and vitamins, making it an ideal snack for soccer players looking to refuel and recover after a game or practice. It's also customizable - feel free to swap in different fruits, milk or yogurt alternatives, or add protein powder for an extra boost.

Recipe: Cottage Cheese and Fruit

Ingredients:

- 1 cup cottage cheese
- 1 cup mixed berries (such as strawberries, blueberries, raspberries)
- 1 tablespoon honey
- 1 teaspoon vanilla extract

Instructions:

1. In a blender or food processor, blend the mixed berries

until smooth.

2. In a mixing bowl, combine the cottage cheese, honey, and vanilla extract.

3. Pour the blended berries into the bowl with the cottage cheese and mix well.

4. Serve immediately, or store in an airtight container in the refrigerator for up to 3 days.

Optional: Add nuts or granola on top for extra texture and crunch.

Recipe: Energy Balls

Ingredients:

- 1 cup of pitted dates
- 1 cup of rolled oats
- 1/2 cup of peanut butter
- 1/4 cup of honey
- 1/4 cup of shredded coconut
- 1/4 cup of chia seeds
- 1/4 cup of chopped nuts (such as almonds or walnuts)
- 1 tsp of vanilla extract
- 1/2 tsp of cinnamon
- Pinch of salt

Instructions:

1. In a food processor, pulse the dates until they are chopped into small pieces.

2. Add the oats, peanut butter, honey, coconut, chia seeds,

nuts, vanilla extract, cinnamon, and salt to the food processor.

3. Pulse until the ingredients are well-combined and the mixture is sticky.

4. Use your hands to roll the mixture into balls, about 1 inch in diameter.

5. Place the energy balls on a baking sheet lined with parchment paper.

6. Chill the energy balls in the fridge for at least 30 minutes to help them firm up.

7. Store the energy balls in an airtight container in the fridge for up to a week.

Recipe: Roasted Chickpeas

Ingredients:

- 1 can (15 oz) chickpeas, drained and rinsed
- 1 tablespoon olive oil
- 1/2 teaspoon garlic powder
- 1/2 teaspoon paprika
- 1/2 teaspoon cumin
- 1/4 teaspoon salt

Instructions:

1. Preheat your oven to 375°F (190°C).

2. Rinse and drain the chickpeas, then pat them dry with paper towels.

3. In a bowl, mix together the olive oil, garlic powder,

paprika, cumin, and salt.

4. Add the chickpeas to the bowl and toss them to coat them in the spice mixture.

5. Spread the chickpeas out in a single layer on a baking sheet lined with parchment paper.

6. Roast the chickpeas in the preheated oven for 20-30 minutes, stirring them once or twice during cooking, until they are crispy and golden brown.

7. Let the chickpeas cool for a few minutes before serving. They can be stored in an airtight container for a few days.

CHAPTER 7:
BREAKFAST

Breakfast is an essential meal of the day, especially for soccer players who need to fuel their bodies for the physical demands of their sport. It is important to break the fast of overnight sleep and provide the body with the necessary nutrients and energy to perform at optimal levels. Breakfast not only provides energy for the body but also helps in improving focus, concentration, and mental acuity.

Soccer players need to eat a breakfast that is high in carbohydrates, protein, and healthy fats to provide energy and help with muscle recovery. Carbohydrates are the primary fuel source for the body during exercise, and a breakfast high in carbs can help maintain energy levels during training and competition. Protein is essential for muscle growth and repair, which is important for soccer players who need to maintain lean muscle mass and recover from the physical demands of their sport. Healthy fats are also important for providing energy and keeping the body satiated.

Skipping breakfast can lead to a lack of energy and focus, which can affect a soccer player's performance on the field. It can also lead to overeating later in the day, as the body craves energy and nutrients. Eating breakfast regularly can also help with weight management and can lead to a healthier overall diet.

10 Breakfast Recipes for Soccer Players:

1. Protein Pancakes: Mix together 1 banana, 2 eggs, and 1 scoop of protein powder. Cook on a non-stick skillet until golden brown.

2. Greek Yogurt Parfait: Layer Greek yogurt, mixed berries, and granola in a jar for a protein-packed breakfast.

3. Egg and Veggie Scramble: Sauté veggies like spinach, peppers, and onions in a non-stick skillet. Add in 2-3 scrambled eggs and cook until set.

4. Avocado Toast: Toast whole grain bread and top with mashed avocado, a sprinkle of sea salt, and a drizzle of olive oil.

5. Overnight Oats: Mix together rolled oats, almond milk, chia seeds, and honey in a jar. Refrigerate overnight and top with fruit in the morning.

6. Breakfast Burrito: Fill a whole wheat tortilla with scrambled eggs, black beans, avocado, and salsa.

7. Smoothie Bowl: Blend frozen mixed berries, Greek yogurt, and almond milk until smooth. Top with sliced banana and granola.

8. Veggie Omelet: Whisk together 2-3 eggs with a splash of milk. Add in sautéed veggies like mushrooms, spinach, and onions. Cook until set and fold in half.

9. Protein Waffles: Mix together 1 scoop of protein powder, 1 egg, 1/2 cup of almond milk, and 1/2 cup of whole wheat flour. Cook in a waffle maker until crispy.

10. Cottage Cheese and Fruit: Top a bowl of cottage cheese with mixed berries, sliced banana, and a drizzle of

honey.

Recipe: Protein Pancakes

Ingredients:

- 1 cup rolled oats
- 1 scoop vanilla protein powder
- 1 tsp baking powder
- 1/4 tsp salt
- 1/2 cup unsweetened almond milk
- 1/4 cup plain Greek yogurt
- 2 egg whites
- 1 tbsp honey or maple syrup
- 1 tsp vanilla extract

Instructions:

1. In a blender or food processor, pulse the rolled oats until they are finely ground.
2. Add the protein powder, baking powder, and salt to the blender and pulse to combine.
3. In a separate bowl, whisk together the almond milk, Greek yogurt, egg whites, honey or maple syrup, and vanilla extract.
4. Pour the wet ingredients into the blender with the dry ingredients and blend until smooth.
5. Heat a non-stick pan or griddle over medium heat.

6. Pour 1/4 cup of batter onto the pan for each pancake.

7. Cook until bubbles form on the surface of the pancake and the edges begin to dry out, then flip and cook until golden brown on both sides.

8. Serve with your choice of toppings, such as fresh fruit, nuts, or a drizzle of honey.

These protein pancakes are a great breakfast option for soccer players because they provide the necessary fuel for a high-energy workout. The oats and protein powder provide complex carbohydrates and protein, which are important for sustaining energy levels throughout a game or practice. The Greek yogurt also adds additional protein, while the egg whites provide a low-fat source of protein. The honey or maple syrup adds a touch of sweetness without adding processed sugar. Overall, this recipe is a nutritious and delicious way for soccer players to start their day.

Recipe: Greek Yogurt Parfait

Ingredients:

- 1 cup plain Greek yogurt
- 1 tablespoon honey
- 1/2 teaspoon vanilla extract
- 1/2 cup mixed fresh berries
- 1/4 cup granola

Instructions:

1. In a small bowl, mix together the Greek yogurt, honey, and vanilla extract until well combined.

2. In a separate bowl, mix together the fresh berries.

3. In a serving glass or bowl, layer the Greek yogurt mixture, mixed berries, and granola until the glass or bowl is full.

4. Serve immediately, or cover and refrigerate until ready to serve.

Optional: You can also add other ingredients to the parfait, such as sliced bananas, chopped nuts, or a drizzle of maple syrup.

Recipe: Egg and Veggie Scramble

Ingredients:

- 2 eggs
- 1/2 cup of chopped veggies (such as spinach, peppers, onions, and mushrooms)
- 1 tablespoon of olive oil or cooking spray
- Salt and pepper to taste

Instructions:

1. Heat the olive oil or cooking spray in a non-stick skillet over medium-high heat.

2. Add the chopped veggies to the skillet and cook for 2-3 minutes until they start to soften.

3. Beat the eggs in a separate bowl and season with salt and pepper.

4. Pour the beaten eggs over the veggies in the skillet and stir gently to scramble.

5. Cook the eggs for 2-3 minutes until they are fully cooked and no longer runny.

6. Serve hot and enjoy!

Note: You can also add a sprinkle of shredded cheese or a dollop of salsa on top of the scramble for added flavor.

Recipe: Avocado Toast

Ingredients:

- 1 ripe avocado
- 2 slices of whole grain bread
- 1 small garlic clove, minced (optional)
- 1 small tomato, sliced
- Salt and pepper
- Lemon juice (optional)
- Red pepper flakes (optional)
- Olive oil

Instructions:

1. Toast the bread slices in a toaster or on a pan until they are lightly crispy.
2. Cut the avocado in half and remove the pit. Scoop out the flesh and put it in a bowl.
3. Add garlic (if using), salt, pepper, and lemon juice (if using) to the avocado and mash it with a fork until it is smooth and creamy.
4. Spread the mashed avocado evenly on the toast slices.
5. Top each slice of toast with sliced tomato.
6. Drizzle some olive oil on top of the tomato slices.

7. Sprinkle some red pepper flakes (if using) on top for an extra kick of flavor.

You can also add other toppings to the toast, such as a fried egg or some smoked salmon, to increase the protein content and make it more filling.

Recipe: Overnight Oats

Ingredients:

- 1/2 cup rolled oats
- 1/2 cup unsweetened almond milk
- 1/4 cup Greek yogurt
- 1 tablespoon chia seeds
- 1/2 teaspoon vanilla extract
- 1/2 cup chopped mixed nuts and dried fruits (optional)

Instructions:

1. In a mason jar or other container with a lid, combine the oats, almond milk, Greek yogurt, chia seeds, and vanilla extract.
2. Stir well to combine, cover, and refrigerate overnight.
3. In the morning, stir the oats and top with chopped nuts and dried fruits, if using.
4. Enjoy chilled.

Optional: If you prefer sweeter oats, add a drizzle of honey or maple syrup before serving. You can also add fresh fruit or berries for extra flavor and nutrients.

Recipe: Breakfast Burrito

Ingredients:

- 2 large eggs
- 1 whole wheat tortilla
- 1/4 cup black beans, drained and rinsed
- 1/4 cup shredded cheddar cheese
- 1/4 avocado, sliced
- 2 tablespoons salsa
- Salt and pepper to taste

Instructions:

1. In a bowl, whisk the eggs and season with salt and pepper.
2. Heat a non-stick skillet over medium heat.
3. Add the eggs and cook, stirring occasionally, until they are scrambled and fully cooked, about 2-3 minutes.
4. Warm the tortilla in the microwave or on a dry skillet.
5. Place the tortilla on a plate and top with the scrambled eggs, black beans, shredded cheese, avocado, and salsa.
6. Fold the tortilla into a burrito, tucking in the sides as you roll it up.
7. Serve immediately and enjoy your protein-packed breakfast!

Recipe: Smoothie Bowl

Ingredients:

- 1 frozen banana
- 1/2 cup frozen mixed berries
- 1/2 cup Greek yogurt
- 1/4 cup almond milk
- 1 tbsp chia seeds
- 1 tbsp honey
- 1/4 cup granola
- Sliced fresh fruit for topping (such as strawberries, blueberries, or kiwi)

Instructions:

1. Add the frozen banana, frozen mixed berries, Greek yogurt, almond milk, chia seeds, and honey to a blender.
2. Blend until smooth and creamy, adding more almond milk if necessary to reach desired consistency.
3. Pour the smoothie into a bowl and top with granola and sliced fresh fruit.
4. Enjoy immediately.

Optional add-ins:

- 1 scoop of protein powder for an extra protein boost
- 1 tbsp of nut butter for added healthy fats

- Spinach or kale for added greens

Recipe: Veggie Omelet

Ingredients:

- 3 eggs
- 1/4 cup diced onion
- 1/4 cup diced bell pepper
- 1/4 cup sliced mushrooms
- 1/4 cup chopped spinach
- 1 tablespoon olive oil
- Salt and pepper, to taste
- Optional toppings: shredded cheese, sliced avocado, salsa

Instructions:

1. In a small bowl, beat the eggs until smooth. Set aside.
2. In a non-stick skillet, heat the olive oil over medium heat.
3. Add the diced onion, bell pepper, and mushrooms to the skillet. Cook until the vegetables are softened, about 5 minutes.
4. Add the chopped spinach to the skillet and cook until wilted, about 2 minutes.
5. Pour the beaten eggs over the cooked vegetables. Use a spatula to spread the eggs evenly over the vegetables.
6. Sprinkle salt and pepper over the eggs.

7. Cook until the eggs are set and no longer runny, about 3-5 minutes.

8. Use a spatula to fold the omelet in half.

9. Top with shredded cheese, sliced avocado, and salsa, if desired. Serve hot.

Recipe: Protein Waffles

Ingredients:

- 1 cup all-purpose flour
- 1/2 cup vanilla protein powder
- 2 teaspoons baking powder
- 1/2 teaspoon salt
- 1 tablespoon sugar or sweetener of choice
- 1 cup milk
- 1/4 cup melted butter or coconut oil
- 2 large eggs
- 1 teaspoon vanilla extract

Instructions:

1. Preheat your waffle maker.

2. In a large bowl, whisk together the flour, protein powder, baking powder, salt, and sugar.

3. In a separate bowl, whisk together the milk, melted butter or coconut oil, eggs, and vanilla extract.

4. Add the wet ingredients to the dry ingredients and mix

until just combined.

5. Spray the waffle maker with non-stick cooking spray.
6. Pour the batter into the waffle maker and cook until golden brown and crisp.
7. Serve with your favorite toppings such as fresh fruit, yogurt, or nut butter.

Recipe: Cottage Cheese and Fruit

Ingredients:

- 1 cup of low-fat cottage cheese
- 1 cup of mixed fresh fruit (such as berries, chopped apples, and grapes)
- 2 tablespoons of chopped nuts (optional)

Instructions:

1. In a mixing bowl, stir the cottage cheese until it is smooth and creamy.
2. Add the mixed fruit to the bowl and stir gently to combine.
3. Divide the mixture into two bowls or serving glasses.
4. Top each serving with a tablespoon of chopped nuts if desired.
5. Serve immediately.

This recipe is high in protein and provides a good source of vitamins and minerals from the mixed fruit. It is a great breakfast option for soccer players who need to fuel up for training or a game. The nuts add a nice crunch and additional protein and healthy fats.

CHAPTER 8:
LUNCH

Lunch is a crucial meal for a soccer player as it provides the necessary nutrients and energy to fuel their performance during training and games. Proper nutrition is key for athletes to perform at their best, and lunch is an important opportunity to refuel the body and replenish energy stores.

A soccer player's lunch should consist of a balanced mix of carbohydrates, protein, and healthy fats. Carbohydrates provide the energy needed to fuel high-intensity exercise, while protein helps repair and build muscle tissue. Healthy fats provide essential nutrients and help maintain a healthy weight.

Skipping lunch or eating an insufficient meal can lead to low blood sugar levels and fatigue, which can negatively impact performance during training and games. Inadequate nutrition can also increase the risk of injury, as the body may not have the necessary nutrients to repair and recover from exercise.

Furthermore, a well-planned lunch can also help a soccer player avoid overeating later in the day. It's important to eat regular, balanced meals to maintain a healthy weight and provide the body with the necessary nutrients to perform at a high level.

Soccer players should aim to eat lunch about 3-4 hours before training or games to allow sufficient time for digestion. A pre-exercise meal that is high in carbohydrates can help maintain blood sugar levels and provide the necessary energy for the upcoming activity. In addition to the physical benefits, lunch also provides a mental break and an opportunity to refocus before the afternoon training session. Eating with teammates can also provide a social benefit, allowing players to bond and connect off the field.

In conclusion, lunch is a critical meal for soccer players and should not be overlooked. Proper nutrition during this meal can help players perform at their best, avoid injury, maintain a healthy weight, and promote overall health and well-being. Soccer players should aim to eat a balanced mix of carbohydrates, protein, and healthy fats and should prioritize their nutrition needs throughout the day.

10 Lunch Recipes for Soccer Players:

1. Grilled Chicken Sandwich: Marinate chicken breasts in olive oil, garlic, salt, and pepper. Grill the chicken and serve on a whole-grain bun with lettuce, tomato, and avocado.

2. Grilled Chicken Caesar Salad: Grill chicken breasts and serve over a bed of romaine lettuce. Toss with Caesar dressing and croutons.

3. Tuna Salad Wrap: Mix canned tuna with diced celery, red onion, and mayonnaise. Spread the mixture onto a whole-grain tortilla and add lettuce, tomato, and avocado. Roll the tortilla tightly and cut into slices.

4. Avocado and Egg Salad: Mix mashed avocado with hard-boiled eggs, diced red onion, and a squeeze of lime juice. Serve on a whole-grain toast.

5. Chicken Burrito Bowl: Cook brown rice and top with grilled chicken, black beans, diced tomatoes, and shredded

cheese. Add a dollop of guacamole and salsa.

6. Veggie Burger: Grill or cook a veggie burger patty and serve on a whole-grain bun with lettuce, tomato, and mustard.

7. Turkey Chili: Brown ground turkey in a pot and add canned tomatoes, kidney beans, chili powder, and cumin. Simmer until the chili thickens and serve with a side of brown rice.

8. Salmon Caesar Salad: Cook a salmon fillet and serve over a bed of romaine lettuce. Toss with Caesar dressing and croutons.

9. Grilled Vegetable Panini: Grill sliced eggplant, zucchini, and red peppers. Layer on a whole-grain panini with pesto and mozzarella cheese.

10. Baked Sweet Potato: Bake a sweet potato in the oven and top with black beans, diced tomatoes, avocado, and salsa.

These lunch recipes are nutritious and delicious, providing soccer players with the energy and nutrients they need to perform at their best during training and games.

Recipe: Grilled Chicken Sandwich

Ingredients:

- 2 boneless, skinless chicken breasts
- 1 tablespoon olive oil
- 1 teaspoon garlic powder
- Salt and pepper, to taste
- 4 whole wheat buns
- 4 leaves of lettuce

- 4 slices of tomato
- 4 slices of red onion
- Mustard or mayonnaise (optional)

Instructions:

1. Preheat grill to medium-high heat.
2. In a small bowl, mix together the olive oil, garlic powder, salt, and pepper.
3. Brush the chicken breasts with the olive oil mixture.
4. Grill the chicken breasts for 5-7 minutes on each side or until cooked through.
5. Toast the whole wheat buns on the grill.
6. Assemble the sandwich by placing a leaf of lettuce, a slice of tomato, and a slice of red onion on the bottom half of each bun.
7. Place the grilled chicken breast on top of the vegetables.
8. Add a dollop of mustard or mayonnaise, if desired.
9. Serve immediately and enjoy!

This grilled chicken sandwich is a great option for a healthy and satisfying lunch for soccer players. It provides a good balance of protein, carbohydrates, and healthy fats, and is easy to make and customize to individual preferences.

Recipe: Grilled Chicken Caesar Salad

Ingredients:

- 2 boneless, skinless chicken breasts

- 1 tablespoon olive oil
- Salt and pepper, to taste
- 1 head of romaine lettuce, washed and chopped
- 1/2 cup croutons
- 1/4 cup shaved parmesan cheese
- Caesar dressing (homemade or store-bought)

Instructions:

1. Preheat grill to medium-high heat.
2. In a small bowl, mix together the olive oil, salt, and pepper.
3. Brush the chicken breasts with the olive oil mixture.
4. Grill the chicken breasts for 5-7 minutes on each side or until cooked through.
5. Let the chicken rest for 5 minutes before slicing it into thin strips.
6. In a large salad bowl, toss together the chopped romaine lettuce, croutons, and shaved parmesan cheese.
7. Add the sliced grilled chicken on top of the salad.
8. Drizzle the Caesar dressing over the salad and toss to combine.
9. Serve immediately and enjoy!

This Grilled Chicken Caesar Salad is a great lunch option for soccer players. It's packed with protein, fiber, and nutrients from the vegetables, and provides a good balance of carbohydrates and healthy fats. It's also easy to make and can be customized with additional toppings or dressing as desired.

Recipe: Tuna Salad Wrap

Ingredients:

- 1 can of tuna, drained
- 2 tablespoons Greek yogurt
- 1 tablespoon dijon mustard
- 1 tablespoon lemon juice
- Salt and pepper, to taste
- 1 whole wheat wrap
- 1/4 cup shredded carrots
- 1/4 cup sliced cucumber
- 1/4 cup chopped bell peppers
- Handful of spinach or lettuce leaves

Instructions:

1. In a medium bowl, mix together the tuna, Greek yogurt, dijon mustard, lemon juice, salt, and pepper.
2. Lay the whole wheat wrap flat on a clean surface.
3. Spread the tuna salad mixture over the wrap.
4. Add the shredded carrots, sliced cucumber, and chopped bell peppers on top of the tuna salad.
5. Place a handful of spinach or lettuce leaves on top of the vegetables.
6. Roll the wrap tightly, tucking in the sides as you go.
7. Cut the wrap in half and serve immediately.

This Tuna Salad Wrap is a great lunch option for soccer

players. It's packed with protein and fiber from the tuna and vegetables, and provides a good balance of carbohydrates and healthy fats. It's also easy to make and can be customized with additional vegetables or toppings as desired.

Recipe: Avocado and Egg Salad

Ingredients:

- 2 hard-boiled eggs, chopped
- 1 avocado, diced
- 1/4 cup chopped red onion
- 1/4 cup chopped celery
- 1 tablespoon chopped fresh parsley
- Salt and pepper, to taste
- Juice of 1/2 lemon
- 2 whole wheat bread slices

Instructions:

1. In a medium bowl, mix together the chopped hard-boiled eggs, diced avocado, chopped red onion, chopped celery, chopped fresh parsley, salt, pepper, and lemon juice.
2. Mash the mixture slightly with a fork to combine.
3. Toast the whole wheat bread slices.
4. Spread the avocado and egg salad mixture over one slice of the toasted bread.
5. Place the other slice of bread on top of the mixture to

create a sandwich.

6. Cut the sandwich in half and serve immediately.

This Avocado and Egg Salad sandwich is a great lunch option for soccer players. It's packed with protein, fiber, healthy fats, and nutrients from the vegetables. It provides a good balance of carbohydrates and is easy to make and customize with additional vegetables or seasonings as desired.

Recipe: Chicken Burrito Bowl

Ingredients:

- 1 boneless, skinless chicken breast
- 1 tablespoon olive oil
- Salt and pepper, to taste
- 1/2 cup cooked brown rice
- 1/2 cup black beans, drained and rinsed
- 1/4 cup diced tomatoes
- 1/4 cup diced avocado
- 1/4 cup corn kernels
- 1/4 cup chopped cilantro
- Juice of 1/2 lime
- Optional toppings: shredded cheese, sour cream, salsa

Instructions:

1. Preheat grill to medium-high heat.
2. In a small bowl, mix together the olive oil, salt, and

pepper.

3. Brush the chicken breast with the olive oil mixture.
4. Grill the chicken breast for 5-7 minutes on each side or until cooked through.
5. Let the chicken rest for 5 minutes before slicing it into thin strips.
6. In a bowl, combine the cooked brown rice, black beans, diced tomatoes, diced avocado, corn kernels, chopped cilantro, and lime juice.
7. Top the rice and bean mixture with the sliced grilled chicken.
8. Add optional toppings as desired, such as shredded cheese, sour cream, or salsa.
9. Serve immediately and enjoy!

This Chicken Burrito Bowl is a great lunch option for soccer players. It's packed with protein, fiber, and nutrients from the vegetables, and provides a good balance of carbohydrates and healthy fats. It's also easy to make and can be customized with additional toppings or seasoning as desired.

Recipe: Veggie Burger

Ingredients:

- 1 can of black beans, drained and rinsed
- 1/2 cup cooked quinoa
- 1/2 cup finely chopped mushrooms
- 1/4 cup diced onion

- 1/4 cup breadcrumbs
- 1/4 cup chopped fresh parsley
- 1 teaspoon garlic powder
- 1/2 teaspoon smoked paprika
- Salt and pepper, to taste
- 2 tablespoons olive oil
- 4 whole wheat buns
- Optional toppings: sliced avocado, lettuce, tomato, onion, ketchup, mustard

Instructions:

1. In a large bowl, mash the black beans with a fork or potato masher.
2. Add the cooked quinoa, chopped mushrooms, diced onion, breadcrumbs, chopped fresh parsley, garlic powder, smoked paprika, salt, and pepper to the bowl with the mashed black beans. Mix until well combined.
3. Divide the mixture into four equal portions and shape each portion into a patty.
4. Heat the olive oil in a large skillet over medium heat.
5. Add the veggie burger patties to the skillet and cook for 5-7 minutes on each side, or until browned and heated through.
6. Toast the whole wheat buns.
7. Place a veggie burger patty on each bun and add optional toppings as desired, such as sliced avocado,

lettuce, tomato, onion, ketchup, or mustard.

8. Serve immediately and enjoy!

This Veggie Burger is a great lunch option for soccer players who are looking for a plant-based protein source. It's packed with protein, fiber, and nutrients from the vegetables and whole grains. It provides a good balance of carbohydrates and healthy fats, and can be customized with additional toppings or seasonings as desired.

Recipe: Turkey Chili

Ingredients:

- 1 tablespoon olive oil
- 1 pound ground turkey
- 1 medium onion, chopped
- 2 garlic cloves, minced
- 1 red bell pepper, chopped
- 1 green bell pepper, chopped
- 1 can (15 ounces) kidney beans, drained and rinsed
- 1 can (14.5 ounces) diced tomatoes
- 1 can (8 ounces) tomato sauce
- 1 tablespoon chili powder
- 1 teaspoon ground cumin
- 1/2 teaspoon paprika
- 1/2 teaspoon salt

- Optional toppings: shredded cheese, sour cream, chopped cilantro, sliced jalapenos

Instructions:

1. Heat the olive oil in a large pot or Dutch oven over medium heat.
2. Add the ground turkey to the pot and cook, stirring occasionally, for 5-7 minutes or until browned and cooked through.
3. Add the chopped onion, minced garlic, chopped red bell pepper, and chopped green bell pepper to the pot. Cook, stirring occasionally, for 5-7 minutes or until the vegetables are tender.
4. Add the drained and rinsed kidney beans, diced tomatoes, tomato sauce, chili powder, ground cumin, paprika, and salt to the pot. Stir to combine.
5. Bring the mixture to a simmer and let it cook for 20-30 minutes, stirring occasionally, until the flavors have melded together.
6. Serve the chili hot with optional toppings as desired, such as shredded cheese, sour cream, chopped cilantro, or sliced jalapenos.

This Turkey Chili is a great lunch option for soccer players. It's packed with protein and fiber from the ground turkey and kidney beans, and provides a good balance of carbohydrates and healthy fats. It's also easy to make and can be customized with additional toppings or seasoning as desired.

Recipe: Salmon Caesar Salad

Ingredients:

- 1 pound salmon fillet
- 1 tablespoon olive oil
- Salt and pepper, to taste
- 1 head of romaine lettuce, chopped
- 1/2 cup Caesar dressing
- 1/4 cup grated Parmesan cheese
- Optional toppings: croutons, cherry tomatoes, sliced avocado, hard-boiled eggs

Instructions:

1. Preheat the oven to 400°F.
2. Brush the salmon fillet with olive oil and sprinkle with salt and pepper.
3. Place the salmon fillet on a baking sheet and bake for 12-15 minutes or until cooked through.
4. Let the salmon cool for a few minutes and then flake it into bite-sized pieces.
5. In a large bowl, combine the chopped romaine lettuce, Caesar dressing, and grated Parmesan cheese.
6. Add the flaked salmon to the bowl and toss to combine.
7. Divide the salad into individual bowls and add optional toppings as desired, such as croutons, cherry tomatoes, sliced avocado, or hard-boiled eggs.

8. Serve immediately and enjoy!

This Salmon Caesar Salad is a great lunch option for soccer players. It's packed with protein, healthy fats, and nutrients from the salmon and vegetables. It provides a good balance of carbohydrates and can be customized with additional toppings or seasonings as desired.

Recipe: Grilled Vegetable Panini

Ingredients:

- 1 zucchini, sliced
- 1 yellow squash, sliced
- 1 red bell pepper, sliced
- 1/2 red onion, sliced
- 2 tablespoons olive oil
- Salt and pepper, to taste
- 4 slices of whole-grain bread
- 1/4 cup pesto sauce
- 4 slices of provolone cheese

Instructions:

1. Preheat a grill or grill pan over medium heat.
2. Toss the sliced zucchini, yellow squash, red bell pepper, and red onion with olive oil, salt, and pepper.
3. Grill the vegetables for 5-7 minutes on each side or until tender and lightly charred.
4. Toast the slices of whole-grain bread.
5. Spread pesto sauce on one side of each slice of bread.

6. Layer the grilled vegetables on top of two slices of bread.
7. Top the vegetables with a slice of provolone cheese.
8. Place the remaining slices of bread on top of the cheese, pesto side down.
9. Grill the panini on a panini press or in a grill pan until the cheese is melted and the bread is crispy.
10. Cut the panini in half and serve hot.

This Grilled Vegetable Panini is a great lunch option for soccer players. It's packed with fiber, vitamins, and minerals from the grilled vegetables, and provides a good balance of carbohydrates and healthy fats from the whole-grain bread and pesto sauce. It's also easy to make and can be customized with additional ingredients or seasonings as desired.

Recipe: Baked Sweet Potato

Ingredients:

- 1 large sweet potato
- 1 tablespoon olive oil
- Salt and pepper, to taste
- Optional toppings: Greek yogurt, chopped chives, shredded cheese, chopped nuts, diced avocado

Instructions:

1. Preheat the oven to 400°F.
2. Wash and dry the sweet potato.
3. Pierce the sweet potato with a fork several times.

4. Rub the sweet potato with olive oil and sprinkle with salt and pepper.

5. Place the sweet potato on a baking sheet and bake for 45-60 minutes or until tender.

6. Let the sweet potato cool for a few minutes before slicing it open.

7. Top the sweet potato with optional toppings as desired, such as Greek yogurt, chopped chives, shredded cheese, chopped nuts, or diced avocado.

8. Serve hot and enjoy!

This Baked Sweet Potato is a great lunch option for soccer players. It's packed with fiber, vitamins, and minerals from the sweet potato and provides a good balance of carbohydrates and healthy fats from the optional toppings. It's also easy to make and can be customized with additional ingredients or seasonings as desired.

CHAPTER 9: DINNER

Dinner is a crucial meal for soccer players as it provides an opportunity to refuel after a demanding day of training or competition. During soccer games, players burn a significant amount of calories and expend energy, leading to depleted glycogen stores in the muscles. To optimize performance and recovery, it is essential to consume a balanced dinner that includes adequate amounts of protein, carbohydrates, and healthy fats.

Protein is important for repairing and rebuilding muscles after exercise, and it also helps to support the immune system. Soccer players should aim to consume at least 20-30 grams of protein per meal, and dinner is an excellent opportunity to do so. Good sources of protein for soccer players include lean meats, poultry, fish, eggs, beans, and lentils.

Carbohydrates are the primary fuel source for soccer players during training and games. Consuming carbohydrates at dinner helps to replenish glycogen stores in the muscles, which can help improve endurance and prevent fatigue. Good sources of carbohydrates for soccer players include whole grains, sweet potatoes, brown rice, quinoa, and fruits and vegetables.

Healthy fats are also important for soccer players as they provide energy and help with the absorption of certain vitamins and minerals. Good sources of healthy fats include avocados, nuts, seeds, olive oil, and fatty fish such as salmon.

In addition to macronutrients, soccer players should also focus on consuming a variety of micronutrients such as vitamins and minerals to support overall health and performance. Vegetables and fruits are excellent sources of micronutrients and should be included in every dinner meal.

Overall, dinner is an important meal for soccer players as it provides an opportunity to refuel and recover after a demanding day of training or competition. A balanced meal that includes adequate amounts of complex carbohydrates, lean protein, healthy fats, fruits and vegetables and hydrating fluids, can help optimize performance and support overall health.

>**Complex carbohydrates:** Complex carbohydrates, such as whole grains, sweet potatoes, or quinoa, are an important source of energy for soccer players. Eating foods that are high in complex carbohydrates can help to support sustained energy levels throughout the day.
>
>**Lean protein:** Lean protein, such as chicken, fish, tofu, or beans, is essential for supporting muscle growth and repair. Eating a variety of lean protein sources throughout the week can help to support recovery and maintain muscle mass.
>
>**Healthy fats:** Healthy fats, such as those found in avocados, nuts, or olive oil, can help to support brain function and overall health. They can also help to keep you feeling full and satisfied throughout the day.
>
>**Fruits and vegetables**: Fruits and vegetables are a great source of vitamins, minerals, and fiber. Eating a variety of colorful fruits and vegetables throughout the week can help to support overall health and well-being.

Hydrating fluids: Staying hydrated is important for soccer players to support performance and recovery. Drinking plenty of water, coconut water, or other hydrating fluids throughout the week can help to keep you feeling energized and focused.

It's important to avoid consuming too much processed food, sugar, or alcohol during the week, as these can have a negative impact on performance and overall health. Eating a balanced diet with a variety of nutrient-dense foods can help to support your body during training and competition.

10 Recipes for a Soccer Player to Eat During the Week:

1. Grilled chicken breast with roasted Brussels sprouts and brown rice
2. Spaghetti squash with turkey meatballs and marinara sauce
3. Turkey and vegetable chili with brown rice
4. Baked Cod with Steamed Vegetables
5. Egg and Vegetable Scramble
6. Grilled Chicken and Pineapple Skewers
7. Grilled Steak with Baked Potatoes and Green Beans
8. Greek-style chicken salad with whole wheat pita
9. Shrimp and Broccoli Stir-Fry
10. Shrimp and Avocado Salad

Remember to prioritize protein, complex carbohydrates, and plenty of fruits and vegetables to help replenish your energy stores and aid in muscle recovery.

Recipe: Grilled Chicken Breast with Roasted Brussels Sprouts and Brown Rice

Ingredients:

- 4 boneless, skinless chicken breasts
- 1 lb. Brussels sprouts, trimmed and halved
- 2 tablespoons olive oil
- 1 teaspoon garlic powder
- Salt and pepper, to taste
- 2 cups cooked brown rice

Instructions:

1. Preheat grill to medium-high heat.
2. Brush chicken breasts with olive oil and season with garlic powder, salt, and pepper.
3. Grill chicken for about 6-8 minutes per side, or until cooked through.
4. While chicken is cooking, preheat oven to 400°F and line a baking sheet with parchment paper.
5. Toss Brussels sprouts with olive oil, salt, and pepper in a bowl until coated.
6. Spread Brussels sprouts out on the prepared baking sheet in a single layer.
7. Roast in the oven for 20-25 minutes, or until tender and browned.
8. Serve the grilled chicken breasts with roasted Brussels sprouts and cooked brown rice.

Recipe: Spaghetti Squash with Turkey Meatballs and Marinara Sauce

Ingredients:

- 1 medium-sized spaghetti squash
- 1 lb ground turkey
- 1/2 cup whole wheat breadcrumbs
- 1 egg
- 1/4 cup grated parmesan cheese
- 1/2 tsp garlic powder
- 1/2 tsp dried oregano
- 1/2 tsp dried basil
- Salt and pepper, to taste
- 1 jar (24 oz) marinara sauce
- Fresh basil leaves (optional)

Instructions:

1. Preheat oven to 400°F.

2. Cut spaghetti squash in half lengthwise and scoop out the seeds. Place the squash halves on a baking sheet, cut side up. Season with salt and pepper, and bake for 35-40 minutes, or until the flesh is tender and easily scraped with a fork. Once done, set aside to cool.

3. In a large mixing bowl, combine ground turkey, breadcrumbs, egg, parmesan cheese, garlic powder, oregano, basil, salt, and pepper. Mix well until fully combined.

4. Form the turkey mixture into small meatballs, about 1 inch in diameter.

5. Heat a large skillet over medium-high heat. Add a small amount of olive oil, then the meatballs. Cook until browned on all sides, about 6-8 minutes.

6. Pour the marinara sauce over the meatballs, reduce the heat to low, and let it simmer for 10-15 minutes, or until the meatballs are fully cooked and the sauce has thickened.

7. Once the spaghetti squash has cooled, use a fork to scrape the flesh into spaghetti-like strands. Divide the spaghetti squash among 4 plates, then top with turkey meatballs and marinara sauce.

8. Garnish with fresh basil leaves, if desired, and serve hot.

Recipe: Turkey and Vegetable Chili with Brown Rice

Ingredients:

- 1 lb ground turkey
- 1 onion, diced
- 3 cloves garlic, minced
- 1 green bell pepper, diced
- 1 red bell pepper, diced
- 1 can kidney beans, drained and rinsed
- 1 can diced tomatoes, undrained
- 1 can tomato sauce

- 1 tablespoon chili powder
- 1 teaspoon ground cumin
- 1 teaspoon smoked paprika
- Salt and black pepper, to taste
- 2 cups cooked brown rice

Directions:

1. In a large pot or Dutch oven, cook ground turkey over medium heat until browned and no longer pink. Drain excess fat if needed.
2. Add diced onion, garlic, green bell pepper, and red bell pepper to the pot with the turkey. Cook until vegetables are soft, about 5 minutes.
3. Add kidney beans, diced tomatoes, tomato sauce, chili powder, cumin, smoked paprika, salt, and black pepper to the pot. Stir well to combine.
4. Bring the chili to a boil, then reduce heat to low and let simmer for 20-30 minutes, stirring occasionally.
5. Serve hot with cooked brown rice.

Optional: Top with shredded cheese, sour cream, avocado, or any other desired toppings.

Recipe: Baked Cod with Steamed Vegetables

Ingredients:

- 4 cod fillets
- Salt and pepper

- 1 lemon
- 4 tbsp unsalted butter
- 2 garlic cloves, minced
- 1 tsp dried oregano
- 1 tsp dried basil
- 1 tsp dried thyme
- 1 cup cherry tomatoes
- 1 bunch asparagus, trimmed
- 1 red bell pepper, sliced
- 1 yellow bell pepper, sliced
- Olive oil
- Salt and pepper

Instructions:

1. Preheat the oven to 375°F (190°C).
2. Rinse the cod fillets and pat them dry with paper towels. Season both sides with salt and pepper, then place them in a baking dish.
3. Squeeze the juice of half a lemon over the cod fillets.
4. In a small bowl, combine the unsalted butter, minced garlic, oregano, basil, and thyme. Mix well, then spread the mixture over the cod fillets.
5. Slice the cherry tomatoes in half, then scatter them over the cod fillets.

6. Cover the baking dish with aluminum foil, then bake for 15 minutes.
7. While the cod is baking, prepare the steamed vegetables. Cut the asparagus into bite-sized pieces and slice the bell peppers.
8. In a large pot or steamer basket, bring about an inch of water to a boil.
9. Add the asparagus and bell peppers to the pot or steamer basket, then cover with a lid and steam for 5-7 minutes, or until the vegetables are tender.
10. Drizzle the steamed vegetables with olive oil, then season with salt and pepper.
11. Serve the baked cod fillets with the steamed vegetables, and garnish with the remaining lemon wedges.

Recipe: Egg and Vegetable Scramble

Ingredients:

- 2 eggs
- 1/4 cup diced onion
- 1/4 cup diced bell pepper
- 1/4 cup diced zucchini
- 1/4 cup diced mushrooms
- Salt and pepper to taste
- 1 tablespoon olive oil or cooking spray

Instructions:

1. In a mixing bowl, beat the eggs with a fork or whisk until well mixed. Set aside.

2. Heat the olive oil or cooking spray in a non-stick skillet over medium-high heat.

3. Add the diced onions and bell peppers, and sauté for 2-3 minutes until they start to soften.

4. Add the diced zucchini and mushrooms, and sauté for another 2-3 minutes until they start to brown.

5. Pour the beaten eggs into the skillet, and use a spatula to mix and scramble the eggs with the vegetables. Cook for 3-4 minutes until the eggs are cooked through and slightly browned.

6. Season with salt and pepper to taste.

7. Serve hot and enjoy!

Optional: You can also add shredded cheese, diced tomatoes, or sliced avocado on top of the scramble for extra flavor and nutrition.

Recipe: Grilled Chicken and Pineapple Skewers

Ingredients:

- 2 boneless, skinless chicken breasts, cut into 1-inch pieces
- 1 pineapple, peeled, cored, and cut into 1-inch pieces
- 1 red bell pepper, seeded and cut into 1-inch pieces
- 1 green bell pepper, seeded and cut into 1-inch pieces
- 1 red onion, cut into 1-inch pieces
- 2 tablespoons olive oil
- 1 tablespoon honey

- 1 tablespoon soy sauce
- 1 tablespoon lime juice
- Salt and black pepper, to taste
- Skewers

Instructions:

1. Preheat the grill to medium-high heat.
2. In a bowl, whisk together the olive oil, honey, soy sauce, lime juice, salt, and black pepper to make a marinade.
3. Thread the chicken, pineapple, bell peppers, and red onion onto skewers, alternating the ingredients.
4. Brush the skewers with the marinade on all sides.
5. Place the skewers on the grill and cook for 10-12 minutes, turning occasionally, until the chicken is cooked through and the vegetables are tender.
6. Remove the skewers from the grill and let them rest for a few minutes before serving.

Recipe: Grilled Steak with Baked Potatoes and Green Beans

Ingredients:

- 1 lb. flank steak
- 4 medium-sized potatoes
- 1 lb. green beans
- 1/4 cup olive oil

- 1 tablespoon garlic powder
- 1 tablespoon paprika
- Salt and pepper to taste
- 1 tablespoon chopped fresh parsley (optional)

Instructions:

1. Preheat your grill to medium-high heat.
2. Scrub the potatoes clean and pat them dry. Pierce them a few times with a fork and wrap each potato in aluminum foil.
3. Place the wrapped potatoes on the grill and cook for about 40-50 minutes, or until they are tender when pierced with a fork.
4. While the potatoes are cooking, trim the ends of the green beans and toss them in a bowl with 2 tablespoons of olive oil, garlic powder, paprika, and salt and pepper to taste.
5. Thread the green beans onto skewers and grill them for about 10-12 minutes, turning occasionally, until they are tender and lightly charred.
6. Rub the steak with the remaining 2 tablespoons of olive oil and sprinkle with salt and pepper.
7. Place the steak on the grill and cook for 4-5 minutes per side, or until it reaches your desired level of doneness.
8. Let the steak rest for a few minutes before slicing it thinly against the grain.
9. Serve the sliced steak with the baked potatoes and

green bean skewers, and garnish with chopped fresh parsley if desired. Enjoy!

Recipe: Greek-Style Chicken Salad with Whole Wheat Pita

Ingredients:

- 1 pound boneless, skinless chicken breasts
- 1/4 cup olive oil
- 3 tablespoons red wine vinegar
- 2 cloves garlic, minced
- 1 teaspoon dried oregano
- Salt and pepper, to taste
- 2 cups mixed greens
- 1/2 cup cherry tomatoes, halved
- 1/2 cup cucumber, sliced
- 1/4 cup red onion, thinly sliced
- 1/4 cup Kalamata olives, pitted and sliced
- 1/4 cup crumbled feta cheese
- 2 whole wheat pita pockets

Directions:

1. Preheat grill to medium-high heat.
2. In a small bowl, whisk together olive oil, red wine vinegar, garlic, oregano, salt, and pepper.
3. Place chicken breasts in a shallow dish and pour marinade over the top. Turn chicken to coat evenly.

4. Grill chicken for 6-8 minutes per side, or until cooked through.

5. While chicken is cooking, prepare salad by tossing together mixed greens, cherry tomatoes, cucumber, red onion, Kalamata olives, and feta cheese.

6. Cut grilled chicken into bite-sized pieces and add to salad.

7. Toast whole wheat pita pockets and cut into triangles.

8. Serve chicken salad with pita triangles on the side.

Recipe: Shrimp and Broccoli Stir-Fry

Ingredients:

- 1 lb. shrimp, peeled and deveined
- 1 lb. broccoli, chopped into small florets
- 1 red bell pepper, sliced
- 1 onion, sliced
- 2 garlic cloves, minced
- 1 tbsp. grated ginger
- 2 tbsp. vegetable oil
- 3 tbsp. soy sauce
- 1 tbsp. oyster sauce
- 1 tsp. sesame oil
- 1 tsp. cornstarch
- Salt and pepper to taste

- Cooked rice, for serving

Instructions:

1. In a small bowl, whisk together the soy sauce, oyster sauce, sesame oil, cornstarch, and a pinch of salt and pepper.

2. In a wok or large skillet, heat the vegetable oil over medium-high heat. Add the garlic and ginger and stir-fry for 30 seconds.

3. Add the shrimp and stir-fry for 2-3 minutes until pink and cooked through. Remove the shrimp from the wok and set aside.

4. Add the broccoli, bell pepper, and onion to the wok and stir-fry for 5-7 minutes until the vegetables are tender-crisp.

5. Return the shrimp to the wok and pour the soy sauce mixture over the top. Stir-fry for another minute or two until the sauce thickens and coats the shrimp and vegetables.

6. Serve the stir-fry over cooked rice.

Recipe: Shrimp and Avocado Salad

Ingredients:

- 1 lb large shrimp, peeled and deveined
- 1 large avocado, diced
- 1 small red onion, thinly sliced
- 1 red bell pepper, diced

- 1 green bell pepper, diced
- 1 jalapeno pepper, seeded and minced
- 1/4 cup chopped fresh cilantro
- 2 tbsp olive oil
- 2 tbsp freshly squeezed lime juice
- 1 clove garlic, minced
- Salt and pepper to taste
- Optional: tortilla chips or lettuce leaves for serving

Instructions:

1. Preheat a grill or grill pan over medium-high heat.
2. In a large bowl, combine the shrimp, olive oil, garlic, salt, and pepper. Toss to coat.
3. Grill the shrimp for 2-3 minutes per side, until pink and cooked through.
4. In a separate bowl, whisk together the lime juice, salt, and pepper to make the dressing.
5. Add the avocado, red onion, bell peppers, jalapeno, and cilantro to the dressing and toss to coat.
6. Divide the shrimp among plates and top with the avocado and pepper mixture.
7. Serve with tortilla chips or lettuce leaves, if desired.

CHAPTER 10: DESSERTS

In general desserts would not be a typical part of any soccer player's regular diet. Desserts are not typically considered healthy, as they often contain high amounts of sugar and fat. However, there are healthier dessert options that can satisfy a sweet tooth without sacrificing health. Here are some ideas for healthy desserts for soccer players:

10 Dessert Recipes for Soccer Players:

1. Fruit salad with a drizzle of honey or a dollop of Greek yogurt.

2. Frozen banana bites dipped in dark chocolate and sprinkled with nuts or coconut.

3. Baked apples topped with cinnamon and a sprinkle of granola.

4. Chia seed pudding made with almond milk and topped with fresh berries.

5. Berry sorbet made with frozen berries and a splash of coconut water.

6. Avocado chocolate mousse made with ripe avocado, cocoa powder, and honey.

7. Greek yogurt parfait with layers of fruit and granola.

8. Homemade fruit popsicles made with pureed fruit and coconut water.

9. Baked pears with a drizzle of maple syrup and a sprinkle of cinnamon.

10. A small serving of dark chocolate with a handful of almonds or walnuts.

Recipe: Fruit Salad with a Drizzle of Honey or a Dollop of Greek Yogurt

Ingredients:

- 2 cups mixed fresh fruit (such as strawberries, blueberries, raspberries, and chopped pineapple)
- 1/2 cup plain Greek yogurt
- 2 tablespoons honey
- 1/2 teaspoon vanilla extract

Instructions:

1. Wash and chop the fruit as desired and place in a large bowl.

2. In a separate bowl, whisk together the Greek yogurt, honey, and vanilla extract until well combined.

3. Drizzle the yogurt mixture over the fruit and gently toss until the fruit is coated.

4. Serve immediately or store in the refrigerator for up to 2 days.

Recipe: Frozen Banana Bites Dipped in Dark Chocolate and Sprinkled with Nuts or Coconut

Ingredients:

- 2 ripe bananas
- 1/2 cup dark chocolate chips
- 1/4 cup chopped nuts (almonds, walnuts, or pistachios)
- 1/4 cup unsweetened shredded coconut

Instructions:

1. Line a baking sheet with parchment paper.
2. Peel the bananas and slice them into 1/2 inch thick rounds.
3. Place the banana slices on the prepared baking sheet and freeze for 15-20 minutes, until firm.
4. Melt the dark chocolate chips in a double boiler or in the microwave, stirring every 30 seconds.
5. Dip each banana slice halfway into the melted chocolate and place back onto the baking sheet.
6. Sprinkle chopped nuts or shredded coconut over the chocolate.
7. Freeze the banana bites for 30 minutes or until the chocolate is firm.
8. Serve immediately or store in an airtight container in the freezer.

Recipe: Baked Apples Topped with Cinnamon and a Sprinkle of Granola

Ingredients:

- 4 apples (Honeycrisp, Granny Smith, or any other baking apple)
- 1/2 cup granola
- 2 tablespoons butter or coconut oil
- 1 teaspoon cinnamon
- 1 tablespoon maple syrup (optional)
- Vanilla ice cream or whipped cream (optional)

Directions:

1. Preheat the oven to 375°F (190°C).
2. Wash and core the apples, leaving the bottom intact so the filling doesn't fall out.
3. In a small bowl, mix together the granola, butter or coconut oil, cinnamon, and maple syrup (if using).
4. Stuff each apple with the granola mixture, pressing down gently to fit in as much as possible.
5. Place the apples in a baking dish and bake for 30-40 minutes, or until the apples are tender and the filling is golden brown.
6. Serve hot with a dollop of vanilla ice cream or whipped cream (if desired). Enjoy!

Recipe: Chia Seed Pudding Made with Almond Milk and Topped with Fresh Berries

Ingredients:

- 1/4 cup chia seeds
- 1 cup unsweetened almond milk
- 1/4 tsp vanilla extract
- 1 tbsp honey or maple syrup
- Fresh berries, for topping

Instructions:

1. In a medium bowl, whisk together chia seeds, almond milk, vanilla extract, and honey or maple syrup.
2. Cover and refrigerate for at least 2 hours, or overnight, until the mixture has thickened and resembles a pudding-like texture.
3. Once the chia seed pudding has set, give it a good stir to break up any clumps and spoon it into individual serving dishes.
4. Top each serving with fresh berries or any other toppings of your choice.
5. Serve and enjoy!

Recipe: Berry Sorbet Made with Frozen Berries and a Splash of Coconut Water

Ingredients:

- 3 cups frozen mixed berries
- 1/4 cup coconut water
- 1 tbsp honey or maple syrup (optional)

Instructions:

1. Add the frozen mixed berries, coconut water, and sweetener (if using) to a blender or food processor.

2. Blend until the mixture is smooth and creamy, scraping down the sides as needed.

3. Pour the mixture into a freezer-safe container and freeze for at least 2 hours or until firm.

4. Once frozen, remove from the freezer and let it sit at room temperature for 5-10 minutes to soften slightly.

5. Scoop into bowls or cups and enjoy!

Optional toppings: fresh berries, sliced almonds, shredded coconut.

Recipe: Avocado Chocolate Mousse Made with Ripe Avocado, Cocoa Powder, and Honey

Ingredients:

- 2 ripe avocados
- 1/4 cup unsweetened cocoa powder
- 1/4 cup honey or maple syrup
- 1/4 cup almond milk
- 1 tsp vanilla extract
- Pinch of salt
- Optional toppings: chopped nuts, berries, or whipped cream

Instructions:

1. Cut the avocados in half and remove the pits.

2. Scoop out the flesh and place it in a food processor.
3. Add the cocoa powder, honey or maple syrup, almond milk, vanilla extract, and salt to the food processor.
4. Blend the mixture until smooth and creamy.
5. Taste and adjust the sweetness as desired.
6. Transfer the mousse to a bowl or individual ramekins.
7. Chill in the refrigerator for at least 30 minutes.
8. Serve with optional toppings if desired.

Recipe: Greek Yogurt Parfait with Layers of Fruit and Granola

Ingredients:

- 1 cup plain Greek yogurt
- 1/2 cup fresh mixed berries (blueberries, raspberries, strawberries)
- 1/2 cup granola
- 1 tablespoon honey
- Optional: sliced almonds or chopped walnuts for topping

Instructions:

1. In a small bowl, mix together the Greek yogurt and honey until well combined.
2. In a glass or jar, layer the yogurt mixture, fresh berries, and granola.
3. Repeat the layers until all ingredients are used up.
4. Top with sliced almonds or chopped walnuts, if desired.

5. Serve immediately or cover and refrigerate until ready to eat.

Recipe: Homemade Fruit Popsicles Made with Pureed Fruit and Coconut Water

Ingredients:

- 2 cups fresh fruit (such as berries, mango, or pineapple)
- 1/2 cup coconut water
- 2 tablespoons honey or agave nectar (optional)

Instructions:

1. Wash and chop the fruit into small pieces.
2. Blend the fruit in a blender or food processor until smooth.
3. Add the coconut water and sweetener (if using) to the fruit mixture and blend again until well combined.
4. Pour the mixture into popsicle molds or paper cups.
5. Insert popsicle sticks into the molds or cups.
6. Freeze for at least 4 hours or until solid.
7. To remove the popsicles from the molds or cups, run them under warm water for a few seconds and gently pull on the sticks.

Recipe: Baked Pears with a Drizzle of Maple Syrup and a Sprinkle of Cinnamon

Ingredients:

- 4 ripe pears

- 2 tablespoons maple syrup
- 1/4 teaspoon ground cinnamon
- 1/4 cup chopped pecans
- 1/4 cup dried cranberries

Instructions:

1. Preheat the oven to 375°F (190°C).
2. Cut the pears in half lengthwise and scoop out the cores with a spoon.
3. Place the pear halves cut side up in a baking dish.
4. In a small bowl, mix together the maple syrup and cinnamon. Spoon the mixture evenly over the pear halves.
5. Sprinkle the chopped pecans and dried cranberries over the pears.
6. Bake in the preheated oven for 25-30 minutes, until the pears are tender and the topping is lightly browned.
7. Serve warm as is or with a dollop of Greek yogurt or vanilla ice cream, if desired.

Recipe: A Small Serving of Dark Chocolate with a Handful of Almonds or Walnuts

Ingredients:

- 1 oz dark chocolate (at least 70% cocoa solids)
- 10 almonds

Instructions:

1. Break the dark chocolate into small pieces and melt in a

double boiler or in the microwave.

2. Stir the chocolate until it's smooth and shiny.

3. Place 10 almonds on a plate or parchment paper.

4. Spoon the melted chocolate over each almond, making sure they are well coated.

5. Allow the chocolate to set by placing the plate in the refrigerator for 10-15 minutes.

6. Serve and enjoy!

CONCLUSION:

In conclusion, a healthy diet is essential for soccer players to perform their best on the field. Soccer is a demanding sport that requires a significant amount of energy and endurance, and proper nutrition is crucial to support these needs. A balanced diet that includes a variety of nutrient-dense foods such as lean proteins, complex carbohydrates, healthy fats, and micronutrients can help fuel the body, improve performance, and support recovery. It is also important for soccer players to stay hydrated and consume adequate amounts of water and electrolytes throughout the day. By prioritizing nutrition and fueling the body with the right foods, soccer players can optimize their performance and achieve their goals on the field.

In addition to the physical demands of soccer, players must also contend with mental and emotional stressors that can impact their performance. Proper nutrition can help support mental health and reduce stress levels, which can ultimately improve performance on the field. Research has shown that consuming foods high in omega-3 fatty acids, such as fatty fish, can help reduce symptoms of depression and anxiety.

Furthermore, soccer players must be able to recover quickly between games and training sessions. Proper nutrition can help support recovery by providing the necessary nutrients to repair and rebuild muscles. Consuming carbohydrates after exercise can help replenish glycogen stores, while protein can aid in muscle repair and growth.

Injuries are also a common concern for soccer players, and proper nutrition can help reduce the risk of injury and support healing. Nutrients such as vitamin C and zinc can help boost the immune system and support tissue repair, while calcium and vitamin D can help support bone health and reduce the risk of fractures.

Overall, a healthy diet is essential for soccer players to perform their best on and off the field. Proper nutrition can support physical and mental health, aid in recovery, and reduce the risk of injury. By making nutrition a priority, soccer players can optimize their performance and achieve their goals.

Printed in Great Britain
by Amazon